2ND EDITION

BASIC BUSINESS ENGLISH

TREVOR B. MITCHELL / BAEK JU HYUN / STEPHEN L. POIRIER

도서출판
청람

Introduction for Students

This book is a beginner-intermediate level business English text designed to improve your English communication skills at work. Each chapter is divided into different sections that deal with various topics related to business English. These include such things as dealing with money, using the telephone, writing e-mails, making appointments, traveling, and holding meetings. The book has translated vocabulary and conversations to make learning English faster for you. We encourage all students to use this book at home and to prepare for each class by studying the vocabulary and conversations before class.

Learning English should be fun, and we hope you have a good time in class. Do not be afraid to ask questions or speak! Making mistakes is normal when you are learning a new language. If you try your best and have fun, we are sure you will learn English. Good luck!

Acknowledgements

Writing an education book is not easy. The authors had the help of many colleagues, students, friends and family. First we would like to thank Professor Lee Hyonho and Michael Putlack of Dongyang Mirae University for their support, advice, and input on the form and content of this book. Lee Hyewon was instrumental with many of the technical aspects involved in putting this book together, and we give her our heartfelt thanks. In addition, we would also like to thank the many teachers we have worked with over the years, especially Rick Dysinger, Kenny Poirier, Tim Binando, and Brad Crawford. Of course, we have learned many things over the years from our Korean students and wish to thank them for being so hardworking and eager to learn.

Contents

Introductions

Section 1 Vocabulary

① Greetings and Small Talk

- accommodations
  n. pl. 숙박(수용)시설, (공중을 위한) 편의, (공공)시설,
  편의의 도모, 대접, 친절심
- auto parts
  자동차부품(automobile parts)
- business card
  명함
- business convention
  비즈니스 컨벤션(비즈니스 대회, 비즈니스 대표자회의,
  정기총회)
- executive
  (사장, 중역, 지배인 등) 간부, 관리직, 경영진, 임원
  *chief executive officer(CEO)
- hotel lobby
  호텔 로비(입구의 넓은 방, 넓은 복도)
- impolite
  a. 무례한, 실례되는
- journey
  n. (보통 육상의) 여행, 여정, (인생 등의) 행로,
  pl. 왕복
- oil company
  석유회사
- pleasant
  a. 즐거운, 기분좋은, 유쾌한 호감이 가는, 상냥한, 쾌활한
- polite
  a. 공손한, 예의바른
- politics
  n. pl. 정치, 정치학, 정무, 관리
- religion
  n. 종교, 신앙(생활), 신앙심
- salary
  n. 봉급, 급료
  vt. …에게 봉급을 주다.
- sales manager
  판매부장

2 Practice your pronunciation of the following expressions.

Informal	Formal
Hi	Hello
How are you?	How do you do?
Nice to meet you.	I'm very pleased to meet you.
What's your name?	May I ask your name?
Where are you from?	May I ask where you are from?
What's your job?	What do you do for a living?
Do you want some coffee?	Would you like some coffee?
How was your trip?	Did you have a pleasant journey?
How's the hotel?	How are your accommodations?

3 Titles

Personal	Business
Mr. – mister	President
Mrs. – missus	Vice President(VP)
Miss – miss	Manager
Ms. – miz	Chief Executive Officer(CEO)

Section 2 Grammar

1 Wh-Questions

A Use these questions when asking for information.

What – **thing** – What is this? It's a pen.

Who – **person** – Who is your teacher? His/Her name is ______________.

When – **time** – When did you wake up? I woke up at 7 o'clock.

Where – **place** – Where are you from? I'm from South Korea.

Why – **reason** – Why are you studying English? I want to get a good job.

Which – **choice** – Which is better, fax or email? I think email is better.

How – **method** – How did you get to school today? I took the subway.

B Use the words in the box to complete the questions below.

What	Who	When	Where	Why	Which	How

1. ______________ do you work?
2. ______________ do you go to sleep?
3. ______________ do you do for a living?
4. ______________ many people are in your team?
5. ______________ is faster, car or subway?
6. ______________ is she?
7. ______________ is it late?

Section 3 Conversation 1 – Making Small Talk

① Try the following conversation with your partner.

A Two men meet at a business convention.

Mr. Smith	Hello. How are you?
Mr. Kim	Fine, thank you. How about you?
Mr. Smith	I'm fine, too. May I ask your name?
Mr. Kim	My name is Kim Sung Soo. What's your name?
Mr. Smith	My name is David Smith. I'm from Canada. Where are you from?
Mr. Kim	I'm from Korea.
Mr. Smith	안녕하세요, 어떻게 지내세요?
Mr. Kim	좋습니다. 고맙군요. 당신은 어떠세요?
Mr. Smith	나 역시 좋습니다. 당신 이름을 물어봐도 될까요?
Mr. Kim	내 이름은 김성수입니다. 당신의 이름은 무엇입니까?
Mr. Smith	내 이름은 데이비드 스미스입니다. 캐나다에서 왔습니다. 당신은 어디에서 왔습니까?
Mr. Kim	나는 한국에서 왔습니다.

At a business convention there are many people to meet. Time is money and business people don't want to waste time. Business people want to know who you are first. Next they want to know what your business is, to see if a connection can be made between both of your businesses. Below is part 2 of the conversation between the two businessmen.

2 Try part 2 of the conversation with your partner.

Mr. Smith	Are you from Seoul, Mr. Kim?
Mr. Kim	No, I'm from Busan. How about you, Mr. Smith?
Mr. Smith	I live in Toronto. What do you do for a living?
Mr. Kim	I'm the president of a small company. We make auto parts.
Mr. Smith	That sounds interesting. I'm a sales manager for an oil company.

Mr. Smith	미스터 김, 당신은 서울에서 왔습니까?
Mr. Kim	아니요, 나는 부산에서 왔습니다. 미스터 스미스, 당신은요?
Mr. Smith	나는 토론토에 살고 있습니다. 직업이 무엇입니까?
Mr. Kim	나는 작은 업체의 사장입니다. 우리는 자동차 부품을 만들고 있어요.
Mr. Smith	흥미롭군요. 나는 석유회사의 판매부장입니다.

A Talk to a partner and answer the questions.

1. Where is Mr. Smith from? Where does he live?
2. Where is Mr. Kim from? Where does he live?
3. What is Mr. Smith's job?
4. What kind of company does Mr. Smith work for?
5. What is Mr. Kim's job?
6. What kind of company does he own?

Section 4 Exercise

1 Polite and Impolite Questions

When you meet someone for the first time, you should be careful when you ask questions. Certain questions are **polite (nice, good)** while others are **impolite (bad, not nice)**. Some people do not like questions about the following subjects: age, body shape, marriage, salary, politics, religion or sex. Subjects that are safe to talk about include sports, news, the weather, likes and dislikes, travel and jobs.

Look at the following questions. Are they polite (P) or impolite (I) when you meet someone for the first time?

1. ______________ Are you married?
2. ______________ You're really fat. How much do you weigh?
3. ______________ How was your trip?
4. ______________ How old are you?
5. ______________ Would you like some tea?
6. ______________ How much is your salary?
7. ______________ Can you play basketball?
8. ______________ Do you go to church on Sundays?
9. ______________ Do you have a boyfriend/girlfriend?
10. ______________ Have you ever tried kimchi before?

Section 5 Conversation 2 – Saying Goodbye

① Try the following conversation with your partner.

Mr. Smith	I have a meeting in five minutes. I must say goodbye.
Mr. Kim	It was very nice to meet you, Mr. Smith.
Mr. Smith	It was very nice to meet you, too, Mr. Kim.
Mr. Kim	Have a nice day.
Mr. Smith	Thank you. You, too. Bye–bye.
Mr. Kim	Goodbye.
Mr. Smith	나는 5분 후에 미팅이 있습니다. 가봐야 합니다.
Mr. Kim	미스터 스미스, 당신을 만나뵙게 되어서 매우 즐거웠습니다.
Mr. Smith	미스터 김, 또한 나도 당신을 만나뵙게 되어서 매우 즐거웠습니다.
Mr. Kim	좋은 하루 되세요.
Mr. Smith	고맙습니다. 당신도 좋은 하루 되세요. 안녕
Mr. Kim	안녕

② Ways to Say Goodbye

Goodbye.

Bye-bye.

See you later.

See you next time.

Have a nice day.

Take care.

It's been good talking with you.

It was very nice to meet you.

Section 6 Exercise – Business Cards

Business cards can be used to introduce yourself. Look at the example and then make your own business card with your information.

David Smith *Sales Manager* Imperial Oil Co.
25 Main St. Toronto, Ontario, Canada
Tel : 1-416-555-7856
Cell phone : 1-416-555- 2312
Fax : 1-416-555-0987
email : dsmith@impoil.com
website : www.impoil.com

Name ______________________ Position ______________________
Company ______________________
Company Address ______________________
Tel ______________________ Mobile ______________________
Fax ______________________ email ______________________
website ______________________

Section 7 Reading

Greetings and Introductions in Different Cultures

Greetings and introductions are different in different cultures. For example, in America, Canada, England, and many other Western countries, people look you in the eye and shake your hand firmly. In France and Italy, people who know each other well sometimes kiss on the cheek. In Russia, men always greet each other with a firm handshake even if they have already met earlier in the day and are very old friends. In Japan and Korea, people bow and don't look at the other person directly. The younger person must bow deeper than the older person to show respect. Sometimes Koreans shake hands, but the older person must be the first to offer a hand. In Thailand, people put their hands together in front of their chest and bow slightly. In Saudi Arabia, people use their right hand to touch their forehead, lips, and chest and make a slight bow while greeting someone. They often shake hands after this first greeting.

다른 문화에서의 인사 및 소개

인사와 소개는 다른 문화에서는 차이가 있다. 예를 들면, 미국, 캐나다, 영국 그리고 많은 다른 서방국가에서는 사람들은 상대방 눈을 보면서 상대방과 굳게 악수를 한다. 프랑스와 이탈리아에서는 서로 잘 알고 있는 사람들은 때때로 볼에 키스를 한다. 러시아에서는 남자들은 비록 그들이 오늘 이미 한차례 만났으며 매우 오래된 친구일지라도 항상 굳은 악수를 하면서 서로 인사를 한다. 일본과 한국에서는 머리를 숙이며 다른 사람을 직접 보지 않는다. 젊은 사람은 존경심을 보여 주기 위해 나이 많은 사람보다 더 깊게 머리를 숙여야 한다. 때때로 한국사람들은 악수를 하지만 나이 많은 사람이 먼저 손을 내밀어야 한다. 태국에서는 사람들은 그들 가슴 앞에 손을 모으고 가볍게 절을 한다. 사우디아라비아에서는 어떤 사람과 인사를 하는 동안 사람들은 그들의 오른손을 이용하여 그들의 이마, 입술 다음엔 가슴에 대고 가볍게 절을 한다. 그들은 이러한 첫 인사 후에 가끔 악수를 한다.

1 Talk to a partner and answer these questions about the reading.

1. In which countries do people shake hands?
2. In which country do you bow?
3. In which country do people kiss on the cheek?
4. In Korea who bows deeper, the older or younger person?
5. Who shakes hands first in Korea, the older or younger person?
6. How do Russian men greet someone?
7. Do Saudi Arabian people shake hands or bow?

Section 8 Review

1 Match the Wh-questions with the best response.

Question	Response
1. What's your name?	A. I live in Busan.
2. Where are you from?	B. He is my coworker.
3. Where do you live?	C. I like pizza.
4. What do you do?	D. I arrived this morning.
5. What do you like to eat?	E. I'm here for the business convention.
6. Who is he?	F. Hi, I'm David Smith.
7. When did you arrive?	G. I am a sales manager.
8. Which is better, coffee or tea?	H. I like coffee.
9. Why are you in Korea?	I. I'm from Korea.
10. Where are you staying tonight?	J. I'm at the Hyatt Hotel.

Section 9 Conversation 3 – Business Cards

① Try the following conversation with your partner.

Tyler	Hello, I'm Tyler Patterson. I'm with the Suncor Group.
Soo Hyung	Hello, Mr. Patterson. It's good to finally meet you in person. I am Soo Hyung Kim. Here is my business card.
Tyler	Thank you. It's nice to meet you too, Mr. Kim. Here is my card also.
Soo Hyung	Thank you, Mr. Patterson. Your card says that your office is located in Vancouver. It's a beautiful city.
Tyler	Yes, it is. We moved our office to Vancouver last year because we have so many new clients in Asia now.
Soo Hyung	I understand. My secretary said you would be bringing the contract with you. Shall we take a look at it and go over the details?

Tyler	안녕하세요. 저는 타일러 패터슨입니다. Suncor Group에 나가고 있어요.
Soo Hyung	안녕하세요. 패터슨 씨. 드디어 직접 만나게 되어 기쁘군요. 저는 김수형입니다. 제 명함 여기 있습니다.
Tyler	감사합니다. 미스터 김. 저도 당신을 만나게 되어 기쁘군요. 제 명함도 여기 있습니다.
Soo Hyung	감사합니다. 패터슨 씨. 당신의 명함을 보니 사무실이 밴쿠버에 있군요. 아름다운 도시죠.
Tyler	예 그렇습니다. 현재 아시아에 새로운 고객이 많기 때문에 지난해에 사무실을 밴쿠버로 옮겼어요.
Soo Hyung	알겠습니다. 비서에 의하면 계약서를 가지고 올거라고 하던데요. 그걸 보고 자세히 검토해 볼까요?

② Talk to a partner and answer the questions about the conversation.

1. What do Tyler and Soo Hyung give each other?

____

2. Where is Mr. Patterson's office located?

____

3. When did Mr. Patterson's office relocate?

____

4. Why did Mr. Patterson's office move?

____

5. Who told Mr. Kim about the purpose of this meeting?

____

6. What is the purpose of this meeting?

____

7. Where are many of Suncor Group's new customers located?

____

Jobs

Section 1 Vocabulary

① Job Names

- **accountant**
  n. 회계원, 경리 사무원, 회계사, 계리사
- **architect**
  n. 건축가, 건축기사
- **assistant**
  n. 조수, 보조자, 보좌인, 점원
- **baker**
  n. 빵굽는 사람, 제빵업자
- **businessperson**
  n. 사업가(남녀 구별 없이 씀)
- **carpenter**
  n. 목수, 대목
- **computer programmer**
  n. 컴퓨터, 계산기, 계산자(者)
- **doctor**
  n. 의사(호칭으로 쓰여)
- **dentist**
  n. 치과의사(dental surgeon)
- **engineer**
  n. 기사, 기술자, 공학자
- **firefighter**
  n. 《미》 소방수(fireman)
- **janitor**
  n. 문지기(doorkeeper), 수위, 《미》 (건물의) 관리인, 잡역부
- **nurse**
  n. 간호사(인, 병)
- **office worker**
  n. 회사원, 사무원, (관청의) 직원
- **police officer**
  n. 경관, 《미》 순경(최하위 계급)
- **receptionist**
  n. 《미》 (호텔 · 회사 등의) 접수원, 응접원
- **secretary**
  n. 비서(= private secretary), 서기관, 비서관, 사무관, (회의)간사
- **soldier**
  n. 육군군인, 군인
- **waitress**
  n. (호텔 · 음식점의) 웨이트리스

2 Job Questions

A These are common questions and answers when people talk about jobs.

What do you do? I'm a/an ______________.

What do you do for a living? I'm a/an ______________.

Where do you work? I work at/in ______________.

Who do you work for? I work for ______________.

Section 2 Grammar

1 Present Simple vs. Present Continuous

Present simple tense is used in three main ways.

A To talk about things that are always true.

The Empire State Building is in New York City.

The sun rises in the east.

The moon goes around the Earth.

B To describe feelings and emotions, likes and dislikes.

I'm tired and hungry.

She is so happy.

I love that business news channel.

C To talk about how often you do something.

I always drink coffee in the morning.

I never take the bus to work.

I often meet customers on the weekend.

2 Sometimes in the present tense we must add “s” or “es” if the subject is “he, she, it”

Example He plays baseball every Saturday.

She watches him play baseball.

3 The Present Continuous Tense is for talking about something you are doing NOW.

I’m writing a letter.

She’s having lunch.

They’re watching TV right now.

Sometimes you can use the **present continuous tense** to talk about the future if there is a **time expression** in your sentence. Check the time expression examples below. You can see how they are used with the **present continuous tense** to speak about the future.

on Wednesday	at 3:00 pm	in 20 minutes	after the movie
next week	tomorrow night	after work	before 5:00 pm

I’m playing baseball **on Saturday**.

Sun Mi is meeting her friends **on Friday night**.

Mr. Lee is eating dinner **after work**.

For more examples of time expressions see Unit 9 of this book.

Section 3 Conversation 1 – What are you doing now?

① Try the following conversation with your partner.

Dave	Hey, Sally, what are you doing now?
Sally	I'm sending some emails to our customers.
Dave	Why are you doing that?
Sally	We are telling them our new address and phone number.
Dave	Good idea. Well, I'm going to lunch now.
Sally	Are you going for Japanese food?
Dave	Yes, I'm going to that new Japanese restaurant.
Sally	Great! I love sushi. Can I join you?

Dave	이봐, 샐리, 지금 무슨 일을 하고 있니?
Sally	지금 막 우리 고객에게 얼마간의 이메일을 보내고 있어.
Dave	왜 그런 일을 하고 있니?
Sally	우리는 그들에게 새 주소와 전화번호를 알려 줄 필요가 있어.
Dave	좋은 생각이군. 그런데, 나 지금 점심 먹으러 가려던 참이야.
Sally	일식 먹으러 가니?
Dave	응 그래, 저 새 일본 식당으로 갈려고 해.
Sally	멋지군. 내가 스시를 좋아하는데. 같이 갈까?

A Talk to a partner and answer the questions.

1. Where is the conversation taking place?
2. What is Sally doing now?
3. What is Dave doing now?
4. Why is Sally sending the emails to customers?
5. Where are they going to have lunch?
6. What kind of food does Sally love?

Section 4 Exercise 1

1 What does she usually do vs. what she is doing now?

The left picture shows what the person usually does. The right picture shows what they are doing now. Write sentences like in the example.

Example

Angela usually wears a suit to work every day.	But today she is wearing a track suit because today she is exercising.

1

Pierre usually ______________ in his bakery.

But today Pierre ______________ because today ______________.

2

Diane usually ______________ in her office.

But today Diane is ______________ because today ______________.

3

Bob usually ______________ his taxi.	But today he is ______________ because today ______________.

4

Sumi usually ______________ an airplane.	But today she is ______________ because today is ______________.

Section 5 Conversation 2 – What do you do? I work for ______

① Try the following conversation with your partner.

Jae Sang	Hi, Mi Hyun. Long time no see.
Mi Hyun	Hi, Jae Sang. What do you do?
Jae Sang	I work for Samsung. I'm an engineer. How about you?
Mi Hyun	I work at a high school. I'm a teacher. I teach math and science.
Jae Sang	That's great. Do you like your job?
Mi Hyun	Yes, it's a lot of fun. I love teaching. How about you?
Jae Sang	I like my job, too. But it's a lot of hard work.
Mi Hyun	That's why they call it work, not play time!

Jae Sang	안녕, 미현. 오랜만이야.
Mi Hyun	안녕, 재상. 무슨 일을 하고 있어?
Jae Sang	나는 삼성에서 일하고 있어. 엔지니어야. 너는?
Mi Hyun	나는 고등학교에서 일하고 있어. 나는 교사야. 수학과 과학을 가르쳐.
Jae Sang	멋지군. 네 직업을 좋아해?
Mi Hyun	그럼. 아주 재밌어. 나는 가르치는 걸 좋아해. 너는 어때?
Jae Sang	나 또한 내 직업을 좋아해. 그러나 아주 힘든 일이야.
Mi Hyun	사람들이 왜 그것을 노는 것이 아니라 일이라고 부르는 이유야!

A Answer the questions with a partner.

1. What is Jae Sang's job?
2. What is Mi Hyun's job?
3. What company does Jae Sang work for?
4. What subjects does Mi Hyun teach?
5. Does Mi Hyun work in a middle school?
6. Does Jae Sang like his job? Why or why not?
7. Does Mi Hyun like her job? Why or why not?

2 Language Point

"I work for" is used to talk about the company, institute or person you work for.

"I work at" or "I work in" are used to talk about the **place** where you work.

I work for Dongyang Mirae University.
I work at a college. (I work in a college.)
I work for Hyundai Electronics.
I work at a factory. (I work in a factory.)

Section 6

Exercise 2

1 Complete the sentences with the present tense or present continuous tense.

1. Bill ______________ in a hospital. (work)
2. Mr. Kim is ______________ home now. (drive)
3. In Korea it usually ______________ in the summer. (rain)
4. I'm ______________ my customers now. (meet)
5. She is ______________ the papers right now. (copy)
6. He always coffee in the morning. (drink)
7. An architect ______________ buildings. (design)
8. I'm ______________ the new software now so I can't help you. (install)

Section 7 Reading

Getting a Job

There are many ways to find a job. First, you need to make a resume. This is a document that shows all of your education and work experience. Then you need to find a job you want. Many people look on the Internet at job boards. Many companies have websites where you can apply for a job. When you find a job you like, you need to send your resume to the company. Then you have to wait. If the company likes you, they will call you for an interview. This is the hardest part. Sometimes there are two or three interviews. Finally, they will tell you if you are hired or not. Do not be unhappy if you don't get a job the first time. Many people fail the first time. Keep trying and you will succeed.

구직

직업을 구하기 위해서는 여러 방식이 있다. 우선, 당신은 이력서를 작성할 필요가 있다. 이것은 당신의 모든 교육과 업무경력을 보여주는 서류이다. 그리고 나서 당신이 원하는 직업을 구할 필요가 있다. 많은 사람들은 인터넷상에서 직업게시판을 본다. 많은 회사들은 당신이 직장에 응모할 수 있는 웹사이트를 가지고 있다. 당신이 원하는 직업을 찾은 경우 그 회사에 이력서를 보낼 필요가 있다. 그리고 나서 당신은 기다려야 한다. 만약 그 회사가 당신을 원한다면, 면접을 보기 위해 당신을 부를 것이다. 이것은 가장 어려운 부분이다. 때때로 두 번 혹은 세 번의 면접도 있다. 마지막으로 그 회사는 당신의 고용 여부를 알려 줄 것이다. 만약 당신이 처음에 직장을 구하지 못한다 해도 불행하다고 여기지 마라. 많은 사람들은 처음에 실패를 한다. 계속 노력하라 그러면 성공할 것이다.

1 Are these statements about the reading True (T) or False (F)?

1. You don't need a resume to get a job. ______________
2. You can find a job on the Internet. ______________
3. Some companies have their own websites. ______________
4. Just call the company, don't send your resume. ______________
5. There is often more than one interview. ______________
6. If you fail the first time you won't get a job. ______________

Section 8 Review

① Match the job with the description.

Job	Description
1. taxi driver	A. fights fires
2. architect	B. answers the phone in a company
3. engineer	C. takes care of sick people
4. receptionist	D. drives a taxi
5. doctor	E. serves food in a restaurant
6. police officer	F. builds something
7. firefighter	G. designs buildings
8. waitress	H. protects people from criminals

② Find the mistake in each sentence and correct it.

1. He is drink tea now. ____________________.
2. I writing my resume now. ____________________.
3. I'm loving pizza. ____________________.
4. Sue works to an office building. ____________________.
5. David is meet his friends this Friday night. ____________________.

Section 9

Conversation – Job Search

① Try the following conversation with a partner.

Samantha	Hi, Jung Mi. What are you doing now?
Jung Mi	I'm searching for a job but I can't decide if I want to work for a big company or a small company.
Samantha	Big companies offer more job security. But getting a promotion at a small company is sometimes easier than at a big company.
Jung Mi	Yes, I agree. Both things are important but I still can't decide. Can you help me?
Samantha	I think the most important thing is getting good experience early in your career. It might take some time before you get your dream job, so getting good experience will help build up your resume.
Jung Mi	That's a good idea. Now I think I know which companies I need to focus on. Thanks, Sam.

Samantha	안녕 정미. 요즘 뭐하니?
Jung Mi	일자리를 구하고 있지만, 대기업에서 일하기를 원하는지 아니면 소기업에서 일하기를 원하는지 결정할 수가 없어.
Samantha	대기업은 보다 고용보장을 제공해 주지. 그러나 소기업에서의 승진은 때로는 대기업에서보다는 더 쉬워.
Jung Mi	그래 맞아. 두 가지 모두 중요해. 그래서 아직 결정할 수가 없어. 좀 도와주겠니?
Samantha	내 생각에는 가장 중요한 것은 네 경력에서 일찍 좋은 경험을 갖는 것이라고 봐. 네가 꿈의 직업을 구하기까지는 시간이 좀 걸릴거야. 그래서 좋은 경험을 갖는 것은 너의 이력을 쌓는 데 도움이 될거야.
Jung Mi	좋은 생각이야. 이제 어떤 회사에 초점을 맞춰야 할지 알겠어. 고마워 샘.

2 Write an answer to each question. Then talk to a partner.

1. Do you have a full time job now? If yes, what is it?

___

2. Do you have a part-time job now? If yes, what is it?

___

3. What job do you want to do after you graduate from university?

___

4. Do you want to work for a big company or a small company?

___

5. What company do many people want to work for in Korea?

___

6. Do you want to work in a Korean company or a foreign company?

___

7. If you could work in another country which country would you like to work in?

___

8. Do you want to start your own company? If yes, what kind of company do you want?

___

9. What is your dream job?

___

Interviews

Section 1 Vocabulary

- apply

  vi. 1. 적용되다, 적합하다(to)

  2. 신청하다, 출원(지원)하다, 의뢰하다, 문의하다, 조회하다(to, for)

- attend

  vt. (…에) 출석하다, (의식에) 참석하다(be present at), (학교 · 교회에) 다니다

  vi. 보살피다, 돌보다(to), 간호하다(to, on, upon)

- deliver

  vt. (물건 · 편지를) 배달하다, (전언 등을) 전하다

  vi. 분만(해산)하다, 낳다

- department

  n. 부문, …부(部), (백화점의) 매장

- develop

  vt. 1. 발달시키다, 발전(발육)시키다,

  2. (자원 · 토지를) 개발하다

  vi. 발달하다, 발전하다, 전개되다, 발육하다(from, into)

- improve

  vt. 개선(개량)하다, 증진하다, 진보(향상)시키다

  vi. 나아지다, 개선되다

- interview

  n. 회견, 대담, 인터뷰, 면접

- order

  n. 1. 순서, 차례

  2. 정돈, 정리, 정렬, (군사) 대형, 대열

- receive

  vt. 1. (제공 · 배달된 것 등을) 받다, 수취하다, 얻다《from》

  2. (교육 · 훈련 · 치료 등을) 받다, 경험하다

  vi. 받다, 수령하다

- resume

  n. 이력서

  vt. 다시 시작하다, 다시 계속하다

  vi. 되찾다, 다시 차지하다

Section 2 Grammar

1 Past Tense

A Regular Verbs

Regular verbs have the same style. They end in d, ed or ied. You can make a verb past tense by doing the following.

B Verb+ d / ed / ied

work–worked	order–ordered	receive–received	deliver–delivered
move–moved	change–changed	start–started	study–studied
develop–developed	upgrade–upgraded	improve–improved	apply–applied
attend–attended			

C Irregular Verbs

Irregular verbs in the past tense do not follow the same style. They have many different spellings and you must study these. Look at the examples below.

get–got	send–sent	see–saw	spend–spent
buy–bought	bring–brought	sell–sold	begin–began
do–did	go–went	make–made	build–built
leave–left	sleep–slept	drive–drove	pay–paid

Section 3 Conversation 1 – Job Search

① Try the following conversation with your partner.

Angela	How is your job search going?
John	I have sent out 20 resumes so far.
Angela	Did you get any interviews?
John	I've got an interview tomorrow for a job at Sparks Electronics.
Angela	That's great news. It's a great company.
John	They are one of the best electronics companies.
Angela	I hope you get the job.
John	Thanks.

Angela	너의 구직은 어떻게 돼 가고 있니?
John	나는 지금까지 이력서 20통을 발송했어.
Angela	면접은 보았니?
John	Sparks Electronics에서 내일 면접을 보기로 했어.
Angela	멋진 소식이구나. 훌륭한 회사야.
John	그 회사는 가장 좋은 전자회사들 중 하나야.
Angela	취업되기를 바래.
John	고마워.

Section 4

Exercise 1

1 Complete each sentence with the correct past tense verb.

study	improve	apply	work	move	order

1. I ______________ for a job at Samsung.

2. I______________ business at DMU for two years.

3. My English ability has ______________ after taking that class.

4. The items were ______________ three weeks ago.

5. After finishing school I ______________ at the company for three years.

6. I spent four years as a sales person and then I ______________ to the marketing department.

Section 5 Conversation 2 – Job Interview

1 Try the following conversation with your partner.

Jenny	How was your job interview?
Jung Hoon	I think it went ok.
Jenny	What did they ask you?
Jung Hoon	They asked me about my education and work experience.
Jenny	Do you think you will get the job?
Jung Hoon	I don't know. Many people applied. They told me they will let us know the result next week.
Jenny	I heard that company expanded. I am sure they will need more workers there.
Jung Hoon	I hope you're right.
Jenny	너의 면접은 어땠니?
Jung Hoon	괜찮았다고 생각해.
Jenny	그들은 너에게 무엇을 질문하였니?
Jung Hoon	그들은 나에게 나의 교육 및 직무경험을 질문하였어.
Jenny	너는 취업될 것으로 생각하니?
Jung Hoon	모르겠어. 많은 사람들이 지원했거든. 그들은 다음 주에 결과를 나에게 알려 준다고 했어.
Jenny	회사가 확장됐다고 들었어. 거기에 일할 사람들이 더 많이 필요할 것으로 확신해.
Jung Hoon	네가 옳기를 바래.

Section 6

Exercise 2

① Write answers for the following interview questions.

1. What did you study at your school?

____

2. When did you graduate?

____

3. Why do you want to work for our company?

____

4. What is your strong point?

____

5. What is your weak point?

____

6. How did you hear about our company?

____

Section 7

Reading

Interview Do's and Don'ts

Sometimes you may not understand a question in an English interview. Do not answer a question when you don't understand it. Just say to the interviewer "Could you repeat the question?" or simply say "I am not sure what you are asking." If the person asking the question is speaking too quickly for you, you can say "Could you speak more slowly?" Make sure you arrive early. Dress nicely and make sure you have extra copies of your resume with you. You should study about the company before the interview. Make sure you speak about what you can do for the company.

면접 시 해야 될 것과 하지 말아야 될 것

때때로 당신은 영어 면접시에 질문을 이해 못할 수도 있다. 당신이 질문을 이해 못할 경우에는 질문에 답하지 말아야 한다. 단지 면접관에게, "질문을 다시 한 번 더 해주시겠습니까?"라고 말하거나 혹은 단순히, "당신이 질문하는 것을 나는 잘 모르겠습니다."라고 말해야 한다. 만약 질문을 하는 사람이 당신에게 너무 빠르게 말을 한다면, 당신은, "좀 더 천천히 말씀을 해 주시겠습니까?"라고 말할 수 있다. 반드시 일찍 도착해야 한다. 옷은 말끔히 차려 입어야 하며, 그리고 반드시 이력서 여분을 가지고 가야 한다. 당신은 면접 전에 동 회사에 대해서 공부해 둬야 한다. 또한 동 회사에 대해 당신이 할 수 있는 것에 대해 분명히 말해야 한다.

Section 8 Review

1 Match the following vocabulary words to their meaning.

Word	Meaning
1. resume	A. not strong
2. deliver	B. to make something better
3. improve	C. a document that you need to get a job
4. receive	D. to go to an event or activity
5. attend	E. to get something from someone
6. weak	F. to bring something to a person

2 Find the mistake and write the correct sentence in the past tense.

1. I having and interview yesterday.

______

2. I don't think I study enough for the last exam.

______

3. My best friend buy a new computer last week.

______

4. The item you were looking for is sell out.

______

5. Mr. Park has drive all night to be here for the meeting.

______

6. June develop a way to reduce our costs by 20%.

______

7. Who was pay for it with their credit card?

______

Section 9 Speaking

1. What kind of job do you want to get?

2. What qualifications do you need to get that job?

3. Is it a difficult job to get?

4. Why do you want to do that job?

5. Have you ever made a resume?

6. What should a good resume have?

Section 10

Conversation 3 – Job Interview

① Try the following conversation with your partner.

Interviewer	We see that you applied for the manager position. Can you tell us about your management qualifications and experience?
Taylor	In university, I majored in management. I graduated in 2016. I also worked as an assistant manager in a coffee shop for one year, so I am familiar with this kind of work.
Interviewer	This job only pays minimum wage. Are you ok with that?
Taylor	I think a minimum wage salary is a bit low for a manager's position. Considering my management qualifications and my work experience as an assistant manager, I know I can do a good job for you. So I think minimum wage would be more suited to a person with no experience.
Interviewer	I agree. If we offer you the job, we could be more flexible on the salary. But we need a person who is flexible with their work schedule. Would you be willing to work at night?
Taylor	Yes I would. I think that is reasonable.

Interviewer	당신은 매니저 직에 지원한 것을 우리는 알고 있습니다. 경영자격증과 경험에 대해 말해줄 수 있어요?
Taylor	대학에서 경영학을 전공하고 2016년에 졸업했습니다. 또한 1년 동안 커피숍에서 부매니저로 일을 했어요. 그래서 이런 종류의 일에 익숙합니다.
Interviewer	이 일은 단지 최저임금만 지급합니다. 그걸로 괜찮아요?
Taylor	최저임금 급여는 매니저 직에 비해 약간 적다고 생각합니다. 저의 경영자격증과 부매니저로서의 업무경험을 고려해 본다면, 당신을 위해 일을 잘할 수 있을거로 봅니다. 그래서 최저임금은 무경험자에 더 적절할거로 생각합니다.
Interviewer	동의해요. 만약 당신에게 일자리를 제공하면, 급여에 대해 보다 융통성을 발휘할 수 있습니다. 그러나 우리는 업무 스케줄에 유연한 사람이 필요해요. 당신은 야간에도 일할 용의가 있어요?
Taylor	예, 할 용의가 있어요. 합리적이라 생각해요.

Section 11 Exercise 3

1 Answer the following questions with your partner.

1. Do you have any work experience?

2. What is the minimum wage in Korea?

3. How much do you think is a reasonable minimum wage?

4. How much vacation time should a worker get each year?

5. Would you like a job helping people?

6. After you graduate what kind of qualification will you have?

7. Would you take a high paying but very stressful job?

8. What kind of job do your parents want to you to get?

9. What kind of job do your parents want you to avoid?

Section 12 Past Time Expressions

1. In job interviews you can use past time expressions to talk about your past education and experience. Look at the past time expressions below.

yesterday	yesterday morning	yesterday afternoon
last night	last Monday	last week
last month	last year	2 weeks ago
6 months ago	5 years ago	for 3 years
in 2015	finished in 2016	on January 13th, 2015
back in the spring	earlier today	recently

Ex) I started working at Samsung **in 2015**.

Ex) I graduated from university **on January 13th, 2016**.

Ex) I worked at the coffee shop **for 3 years**.

2 Answer the questions using past time expressions.

1. When did you graduate from high school?

____

2. When did you enter university?

____

3. When did you finish your military service?

____

4. When did you buy your smart phone?

____

5. When was the last time you applied for a job?

____

6. When was the last time you had an interview?

____

Office Talk

Section 1 Vocabulary

- ASAP(as soon as possible)
  가능한한 빨리
- cabinet
  n. 장식장, 진열장, 작은 진열실
- cooler
  n. 냉각기
- drawer
  n. 서랍
- envelope
  n. 봉투
- fax machine
  팩스기계
- filing cabinet
  n. 서류 정리용 캐비닛
- fridge
  n.《구어》 냉장고
- garbage can
  n. 쓰레기통
- ink cartridge
  n. 잉크 카트리지
- mail box
  n.《미》 우체통, 포스트
- printer
  n. 인쇄기, (컴퓨터) 프린터
- photocopier
  n. 사진 복사기
- paper clip
  n. 종이 집게, 클립
- refill
  vt. 다시 (꽉) 채우다, 보충하다
  vi. 다시 차다
  n. 새보충물, (볼펜 등의) 바꾸어 쓰는 심
- scanner
  스캐너
- stapler
  n. 제책기(機), 스테이플러

Section 2

Grammar

① Command Words

Command words are often used in office situations. They are commonly used when the office is very busy. Workers often don't have time to be formal or use long or more polite statements. They are not being rude to each other; they just do this to save time when everyone is busy. You can use command words in the office when you are very busy and don't have time to talk more. People will understand. Look at these examples.

Pass me the stapler.

Get more A4 paper.

Bring that book.

Look under the cabinet.

Turn off the lights.

Section 3

Conversation 1 – Commands

① Try the following conversation with your partner.

Kenny	Sue, bring me the stapler and the envelopes.
Sue	Sure, where are they?
Kenny	I think they are on Bob's desk.
Sue	They are not on Bob's desk.
Kenny	Well I don't see them. Check Jill's desk.
Sue	Here they are. They were next to her telephone.
Kenny	Thanks.
Sue	No problem.

Kenny	수, 나에게 스태플러와 편지봉투를 가져다 주겠니?
Sue	그래, 그것들이 어디에 있지?
Kenny	밥의 책상 위에 있다고 생각해.
Sue	밥의 책상 위에 없어.
Kenny	글쎄, 그것들이 보이지 않아. 질의 책상 위에 있으려나.
Sue	여기에 있군. 그녀의 전화기 옆에 있었어.
Kenny	고마워.
Sue	천만에.

Section 4

Exercise 1

1 Following directions – how to do something

The following are instructions from the boss telling a worker how to open a business every morning. They are not in the correct order. List the directions in the correct order they should happen.

1. ______________ Wait for the customers to come in.

2. ______________ Unlock and open the front gate of the store at 8:30 am.

3. ______________ Turn on the lights. Be careful, it's dark in there.

4. ______________ Turn on the heater because the store is cold in the morning.

5. ______________ Put the open sign in the window after it gets warmer.

6. ______________ Unlock the front door.

Section 5

Conversation 2 – Finishing a Task

① Try the following conversation with your partner.

Boss	Harris, could I speak with you?
Harris	Yes, sir.
Boss	Have you completed the work on the Choi account?
Harris	I am almost finished with it. It should be ready in about 30 minutes.
Boss	Get it to the Marketing Department ASAP. They are waiting for it.
Harris	I'll get it done and send it to them, sir.

Boss	해리스, 당신과 얘기해도 될까?
Harris	예.
Boss	최의 계정에 관한 일을 완료하였어?
Harris	그 일을 거의 끝냈습니다. 약 30분 내에 준비되도록 하겠습니다.
Boss	가능한한 빨리 마케팅부에 도착되도록 하게. 기다리고 있는 중이거든.
Harris	그 일을 끝내고 보내도록 하겠습니다.

Section 6 Exercise 2

1 Find the mistake(s) and write the correct sentence.

1. Found the Nelson account and putting it on my desk.

2. Passing that stapler to me.

3. Took this to the seventh floor and give it to Hye Won.

4. Sent this email to Derek as soon as possible.

5. Bringing the file and met me in the front lobby in 20 minutes.

Section 7 Reading

In busy office situations you can use command words to ask for things quickly. Something you can practice is the use of the expressions **"thank you"** and **"please."** When asking for something or telling a person to do something, you can say "please" at the end of the statement to be more polite.

Example A : Pick up the report from Susan in marketing **please**.
B : Sure, no problem.
A : **Thank you**.

Example A : Can you reach that item on top **please**?
B : Ok, here it is.
A : **Thank you**.

Using **please** at the end of your statement or question is more polite. If you use it, people will be happier to help you. Also never forget to say **thank you**. It shows the person you appreciate what they have done for you and it helps make relationships in the office better.

바쁜 업무 상황에서는 당신은 어떤 일들을 빨리 요구하기 위해 명령어를 사용할 수 있다. 당신이 실행할 수 있는 것은 "thank you" 그리고 "please"라는 표현을 이용하는 것이다. 무엇을 요구하거나 또는 어떤 사람에게 그 무엇인가를 해 달라고 부탁할 경우, 당신은 진술의 말미에 보다 공손하게 "please"라고 말할 수 있다.

예 A : 수산으로부터 마케팅 보고서를 좀 찾아오세요.
B : 예, 알았어요.
A : 고마워요.

예 A : 상단에 있는 그 품목을 좀 건네 주시겠어요?
B : 좋아요, 여기 있어요.
A : 고마워요.

당신의 진술 또는 질문의 말미에 "please"를 사용하는 것은 보다 공손하다. 만약 당신이 그것을 사용한다면, 사람들은 당신을 도우는 데 보다 행복해 할 것이다. 또한 "Thank you"라고 말하는 것을 잊어서는 안 된다. 그것은 당신이 감사하는 사람에게 그들이 당신을 위해 했던 것을 보여주며 그리고 그것은 사무실의 관계를 보다 더 좋게 만드는 것을 도와준다.

Section 8 Review

Imagine you are in a busy office. You need some items. Make sentences using command words for each situation.

1. You need to borrow a pen from a person at a desk beside you.

____

2. You want your co–worker to send an email to the sales department.

____

3. You want the secretary to make 20 copies of a report for you.

____

4. The office printer needs to be refilled with paper.

____

5. The office cabinet has to be unlocked.

____

Section 9 Speaking

1 Ask and answer these questions with your partner.

1. Are you busy these days?
2. What have you been working on recently?
3. Have you ever had a job? What was it? Did you like it?
4. What job do you want in the future?
5. Do you want to work in an office or somewhere else?

Section 10 Excuse Me & Pardon Me

When you want to politely start a conversation with someone, ask a person a question, or get a person's attention, there are two great expressions you can use to open the conversation. They are **excuse me** and **pardon me.**

When speaking to a person you don't know, use the expressions in formal style.

Ex) **Excuse me**, sir. Could you tell me where the marketing department is please?
Ex) **Pardon me**, miss. Do you know where I can find the assistant manager?

When speaking to a person you know, you can use the expressions with an informal style.

Ex) **Excuse me**, Sarah. Can you take a look at this?
Ex) **Pardon me**, Min Su. Do you know the password for this computer?

Section 11 Asking Formal Questions

1 Ask polite formal style questions using excuse me or pardon me for each situation.

1. You want to know where the CEO's office is located.

2. You would like a secretary to call a taxi for you.

3. You want to know where the restroom is.

4. You would like to ask a security guard when the parking lot closes for the night.

5. You want to know why your meeting with the marketing manager has been cancelled.

6. You want a secretary to reschedule your meeting with the manager to Friday the 15th.

7. You are thirsty and would like a cup of water.

Section 12 Asking Informal Questions

1 Ask polite informal style questions using excuse me or pardon me for each situation.

1. Ask Hannah if you can borrow her pen.

2. Ask Matthew to call the advertising department and get an update on their plan.

3. Ask Jessica if she knows when the delivery will arrive.

4. Ask Samantha to help you.

5. Ask Austin if he could change the bottle on the water cooler.

6. Ask Chris if he would like to join you for lunch.

7. Ask Jung Hoon to pick up the delivery on the 1st floor.

UNIT 5 Money

Section 1 Vocabulary

- **ATM/bank machine**
  n. (금융)현금자동입금 · 지급기
- **change**
  n. 거스름돈, 잔돈(=small change)
  vt. 환전하다, 잔돈으로 바꾸다, (수표 · 어음을) 현금으로 바꾸다
- **check**
  n. 《미》 수표(《영》 cheque) 계산서(《영》 bill), 청구서, 영수증
- **cost**
  n. 1. (제작 · 공사 등의) 비용, (생산)원가, 경비
  2. (상품 · 서비스에 대한) 대가, 값, 가격
- **counter sign**
  n. 1. 군호(password), 응답 신호
  2. 부서, 연서
- **credit card**
  n. 신용카드
- **debit card**
  n. 데빗 카드(은행 예금을 직접 인출 · 예입할 수 있는 카드)
- **decimal point**
  n. 소수점(point)
- **deposit**
  vt. (돈을) 맡기다, 예금하다, 공탁하다(in, with),
  n. 맡김, 기탁, 적립금, 증거금, 기탁물, 전셋돈, 공탁금, 예금(액), 보석금
- **direct deposit**
  n. (급료 등의) 은행계좌불입제도
- **dime**
  n. 10센트 동전
- **dollar**
  n. a 달러, 1달러 화폐
- **exchange**
  n. 교환, 주고받음, 교역
  vt. 교환하다, 환전하다(for)
- **interest rate**
  n. 금리, 이율

- **loss**

n. 1. 분실, 유실, 손실, 손해
 2. 손실물, 손실 액수

- **nickel**

n. 5센트짜리 백통화

- **one half**

이분의 일, 반절

- **one quarter**

사분의 일

- **passbook/bankbook**

n. 은행(예금) 통장

- **penny/cent**

n. 1페니, 페니화, 영국의 화폐 단위/센트, 1센트 동화

- **percent**

n. 퍼센트, 백분

- **profit**

n. (금전상의) 이익, 이득, 이윤, 흑자, 벌이

vt. 《문어》 …의 이익(득, 도움)이 되다

vi. 이익을 얻다, 도움이 되다, 득보다, 얻는 바가 있다(by, from)

- **quarter**

n. 1. 4분의 1, 1/4(a fourth)
 2. 4분의 1달러(=25cents)

- **service charge**

n. (호텔 등의) 서비스료

- **travelers check**

n. 여행자수표

- **withdraw**

(물건 등을) 꺼내다, (예금 등을)(은행으로부터) 인출하다

Section 2 Pronounciation

In the office or in business you have to work with lots of numbers. Not pronouncing a number correctly can result in a misunderstanding and cost a company big money. Mistakes with dates, times, amounts, measurements and money can get a worker in a lot of trouble. Take your time and be sure to pronounce the numbers correctly.

1 Example : Thirteen-Thirty

Notice that the spelling and pronunciation is very similar. It is very easy to not pronounce numbers like that correctly in conversation or on the phone.

It is important not to mispronounce numbers in business. Practice pronouncing the numbers listed below.

Twelve – Twenty
Thirteen – Thirty
Fourteen – Forty
Fifteen – Fifty
Sixteen – Sixty
Seventeen – Seventy
Eighteen – Eighty
Nineteen – Ninety

Section 3 Conversation 1 – Exchanging Money

1 Try the following conversation with your partner.

Banker	Good afternoon, sir. How can I help you?
Keun	I'd like to exchange 300 U.S. dollars please.
Banker	Will that be cash or travelers checks?
Keun	That will be travelers checks.
Banker	Ok, you will need to counter sign each check. I will also need to see your passport.
Keun	Sure, no problem. Here you are.
Banker	Would you like that in twenties or fifties?
Keun	Twenties please. Thank you very much.
Banker	You're welcome.

Banker	안녕하세요. 무엇을 도와 드릴까요?
Keun	미화 300불을 좀 바꾸고 싶습니다.
Banker	현금입니까? 또는 여행자수표입니까?
Keun	여행자수표가 되겠습니다
Banker	좋아요. 매 수표에 서명이 필요합니다. 당신의 여권을 보여 주셔야 합니다.
Keun	예, 좋아요. 여기 있습니다.
Banker	20불짜리를 원하세요 또는 50불짜리를 원하세요?
Keun	20불짜리로 부탁합니다. 대단히 고맙습니다.
Banker	천만에요.

Section 4 Pronounciation

① Pronouncing Large Numbers

It is important to remember that English and Korean speaking people organize numbers differently. Large Korean numbers are often organized in groups of 10,000, while large English numbers are often organized in groups of 1000.

Ex) 10,000 – ten thousand
Ex) 74,000 – seventy four thousand
Ex) 189,000 – one hundred eighty nine thousand

Try practicing the numbers listed below.

1 : one
10 : ten
100 : one hundred
1,000 : one thousand
10,000 : ten thousand
100,000 : one hundred thousand
1,000,000 : one million
10,000,000 : ten million
100,000,000 : one hundred million
1,000,000,000 : one billion

② Pronouncing Difficult Numbers

39,124 : thirty nine thousand, one hundred twenty four
1,890,000 : one million, eight hundred ninety thousand
19,990,000 : nineteen million, nine hundred ninety thousand
395,515,800 : three hundred ninety five million, five hundred fifteen thousand, eight hundred

3 Practice the prices in won.

₩10 : ten won

₩50 : fifty won

₩100 : one hundred won

₩500 : five hundred won

₩1,000 : one thousand won

₩5,000 : five thousand won

₩10,000 : ten thousand won

₩50,000 : fifty thousand won

₩100,000 : one hundred thousand won

₩1,000,000 : one million won

₩10,000,000 : ten million won

₩100,000,000 : one hundred million won

4 Practice the prices in dollars and cents.

$0.01 : one cent (penny)

$0.05 : five cents (nickel)

$0.10 : ten cents (dime)

$0.25 : twenty five cents (quarter)

$0.50 : fifty cents

$1.00 : one dollar

$1.99 : one dollar, ninety nine cents / dollar ninety nine

$2.00 : two dollars

$5.00 : five dollars

$5.75 : five dollars, seventy five cents / five seventy five

$10.00 : ten dollars

$20.00 : twenty dollars

$50.00 : fifty dollars

$100.00 : one hundred dollars

Another informal expression that is sometimes used to refer to dollars is the word "**bucks**."

Ex) $100 : one hundred bucks
Ex) $750 : seven hundred fifty bucks
Ex) $1,000,000 : one million bucks

When English speaking people use the expression **bucks** they almost never use it together with the word **cents**. If you said 27 bucks fifty cents it would sound strange to them so you should avoid using the word **bucks** and **cents** together.

5 Answer the questions together with a partner.

1. How much does it cost you to travel to school each day?

___

2. How much does your favorite pizza cost?

___

3. What is the most expensive thing you ever bought? How much did you pay for it?

___

4. How much did you spend on your mother's birthday gift?

___

Section 5 Exercise 1

① Try to write each of the following numbers in words.

1. ₩160,000

2. $375,000

3. $19.99

4. 75%

5. ₩25,432,900

6. 99.5%

7. 1/4

8. 1/2

Section 6 Speaking

1 Ask and answer the following questions with your partner.

1. Do you have a purse or a wallet?
2. How much money do you have with you right now?
3. Do you use a credit card?
4. What is your favorite discount or point card?
5. Why do you like that card the most?

Section 7 Conversation 2 – Buying

① Try the following conversation with your partner.

Tim	Burk's Electronics, Tim speaking. How can I help you?
Hyun min	Good morning Tim. I'm calling to check on the price of your printers.
Tim	Yes, we have only one printer in stock. It's on sale for $129.99.
Hyun min	Does it have printing and scanning functions?
Tim	Yes, it does. It also comes with a 2 year warranty.
Hyun min	Great, I'll drop by later to take a closer look.
Tim	Ok, we close at 9:00pm. Just come to the customer service desk and ask for Tim.
Hyun min	Ok, I'll see you around 7:30 this evening.

Tim	Burk? Electronics, 팀입니다. 뭘 도와 드릴까요?
Hyun min	안녕하세요 팀. 귀사의 프린트 가격에 대해 알아보려고 전화했습니다.
Tim	잘 하셨습니다. 당사는 재고 프린트 단 한 대가 있습니다. 129불 99센트에 판매하고 있습니다.
Hyun min	프린트 및 스캔 기능을 가지고 있습니까?
Tim	예, 그렇습니다. 2년간 보증합니다.
Hyun min	좋아요, 자세히 보기 위해 나중에 방문하겠습니다.
Tim	좋아요, 당사는 저녁 9시에 문을 닫습니다. 고객서비스 데스크로 오셔서 팀을 찾으시기 바랍니다.
Hyun min	좋아요, 오늘 저녁 7시 30분경에 뵙겠습니다.

Section 8 Exercise 2

1 Reading graphs and charts

A Use the words in the box to describe what is happening in each of the graphs below.

declined	remained unchanged	rose and leveled off	dropped suddenly	fell sharply
rose sharply	fell sharply and then stabilized	fluctuated		

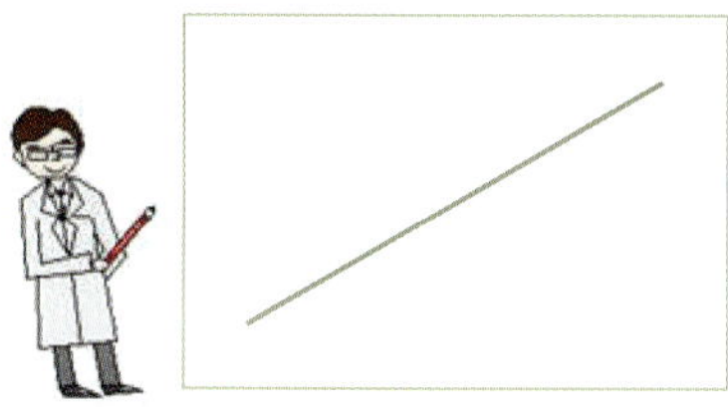

Sales

Sales increased.

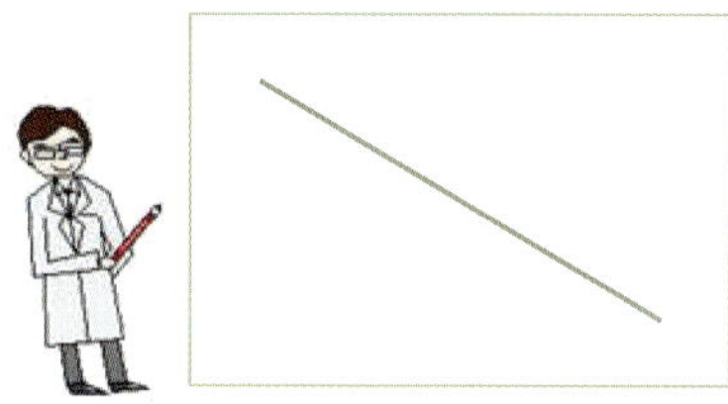

Costs

____

Prices

____

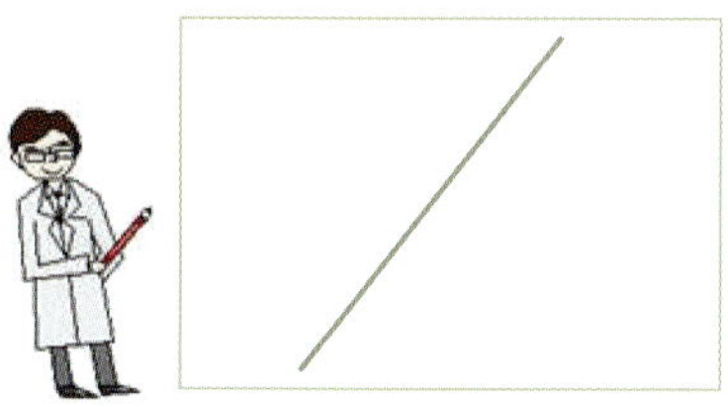

Demand

____

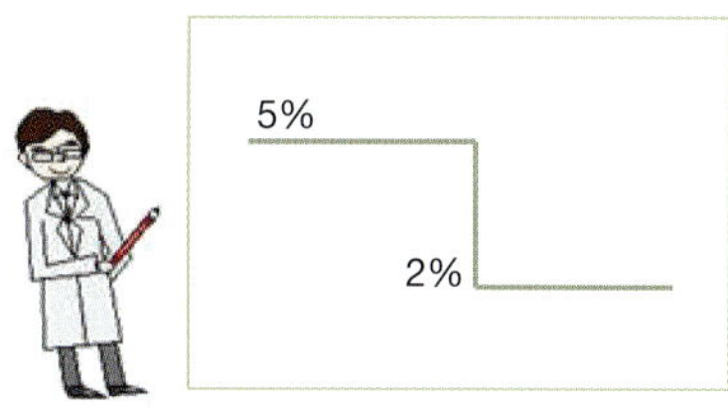

Interest Rate

____

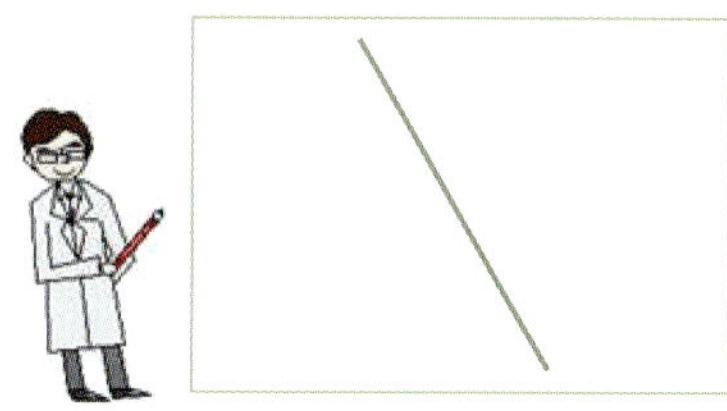

Inflation

____

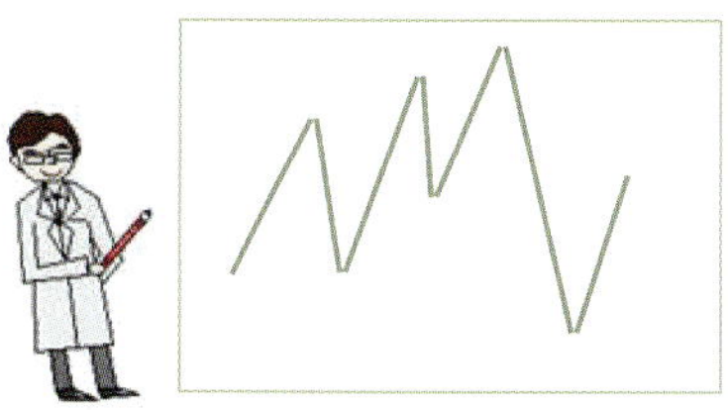

Exchange Rate

____

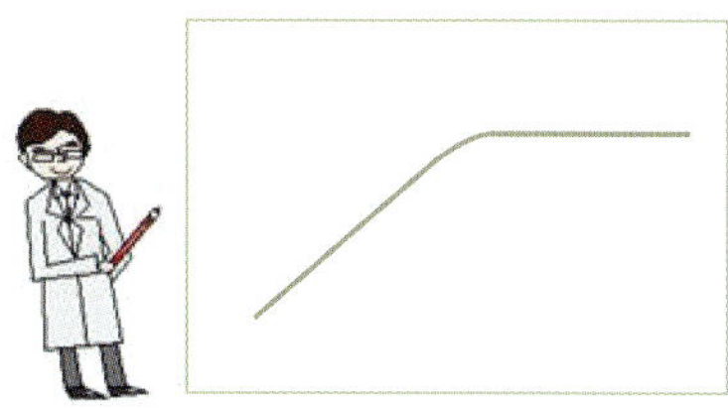

Imports

____

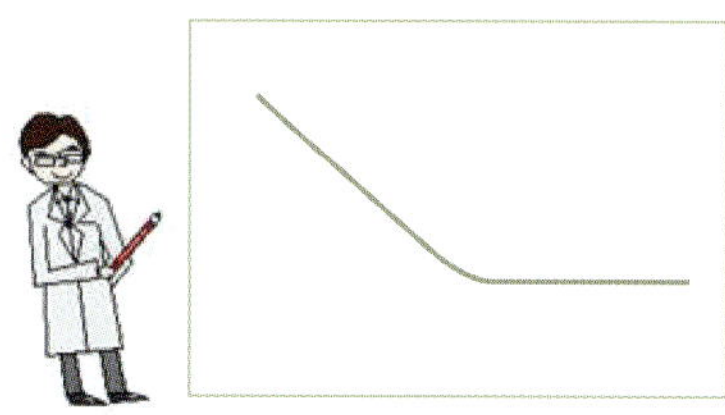

Exports

____

Reading

The Origin of Coins and Paper Money

People started making coins from gold and silver. Coins first appeared in Turkey over 2700 years ago. But gold and silver were not the only metals used for making coins. People also made coins from copper and brass. Coins were very convenient if you wanted to buy something cheap. If you wanted to buy something expensive, you would need many coins. This could be very heavy to carry. It was very difficult to travel long distances because you needed to carry so many coins.

The Chinese were the first people to come up with the idea of using paper money. They thought of this idea about 1000 years ago. The idea of using paper money took a long time to be accepted throughout the world. But the use of paper money made shopping, travel and life in general a lot easier for people. It was a small invention that forever changed the world of business.

경화(硬貨)와 지폐의 기원

사람들은 금과 은으로부터 경화를 만들기 시작했다. 경화는 2700여 년전에 터키에서 출현했다. 그러나 금과 은이 경화를 만들기 위해 사용된 유일한 금속은 아니었다. 사람들은 또한 구리와 놋쇠로 경화를 만들기도 했다. 경화는 당신이 값이 싼 어떤 것을 구매하기를 원한다면 매우 편리하다. 당신이 값이 비싼 어떤 것을 구매하기를 원한다면, 많은 경화가 필요할 것이다. 운반하기에 매우 무거웠을 것이다. 먼 거리를 여행하는 것은 매우 어려웠는데 왜냐하면 아주 많은 경화가 필요했기 때문이었다.

중국사람들은 지폐사용의 아이디어를 처음 생각해 낸 사람들이었다. 그들은 약 천년 전에 이러한 아이디어를 생각했다. 지폐사용의 아이디어는 전 세계를 통하여 받아들여지는 데는 오랜 시간이 걸렸다. 그러나 지폐의 사용은 사람들에게 쇼핑, 여행 및 생활을 대체로 아주 쉽게 해 주었다.

Answer the questions about the story above.

1. What metals were used to make coins?

2. Where were coins first used?

3. Who were the first people to make paper money?

4. Why did people like paper money?

Section 10 Review

Talk to your partner and answer the following questions.

1. How much did your English text book cost?
2. Where can you exchange U.S. dollars?
3. What do you have to counter sign?
4. How can you deposit money in the bank when it's 8:00 pm?
5. How much is the service charge when you withdraw money from a bank machine?
6. How much money do you usually spend in one day?
7. What do you like to spend money on?
8. If you had a lot of money, what would you buy?

Buying and Selling

Section 1 Vocabulary

2 for 1 Sale
하나 값에 두 개를 팔다

- buy
  vt. 사다, 구입하다(opp. sell)
  vi. 사다, 쇼핑하다, 사는 쪽이 되다
  n. 사기, 구입(purchase)
- buy 1 get 1 free
  하나를 사면 하나가 무료
- cheap
  a. 싼, 값이 싼, (가게 등이) 싸게 파는, 물건이 싼
  ad. 싸게
- clearance sale
  창고정리판매, 염가판매
- discount
  vt. 할인하다(게시에서는 10% OFF 또는 SAVE 10% 등으로 표기함)
  vi. 할인하다
  n. 할인
- exchange (item)
  n. 교환, 주고받음, 교역, 교환하다, 환전하다(for)
- expensive
  a. 값비싼, 비용이 많이 드는, 고가의, 사치스러운
- expire
  vi. (계약 · 보증 등이) 만기가 되다, (기간이) 끝나다, (자격 등이) 소멸하다
- fire sale
  팔다 남은 물건의 방매(특매)
- going out of business sale
  점포정리판매, 폐점세일
- inflation
  n. 인플레이션, 통화 팽창, (물가 등의) 폭등
- rebate
  (지불한 금액의 일부를) 환불하다, (…에게) 환불해주다, 리베이트를 주다
- receipt
  n. 영수증
- refund
  vt. (금전을) 갚다, 반제(상환)하다, 환불하다
  vi. 반제하다
  n. 반제, 환불, 상환, 상환액
- sales tax
  n. 판매(영업)세
- sale
  n. 판매, 매각, 매도(selling), 매매, 거래
- selection
  n. 선발, (신중한) 선택, 정선(choice)
- sell
  vt. 팔다, 매도하다, 매각하다(opp. buy)
  vi. (사람이) 팔다, 장사하다, 팔러가다, 팔려고 하다
  n. 판매(술)
- sold out
  a. 매진된
- tax
  n. 세, 세금, 조세
- warranty
  n. 보증(이 되는 것), 담보물건
  vt. 1. 정당화하다(justify)
  2. 《구어》 보증하다, 단언하다, 장담하다

Section 2 Grammar

1 Modal Verbs

Modal verbs are special verbs that act differently than normal verbs. Modal verbs include: **would, should, could, can, may, might, must** and **will**. Modal verbs do not add "s."

Would : offers and requests
Should : giving advice
Could : possibilities and requests
Can : ability and permission
May/Might : possibilities
Must : obligation/requirement
Will : requests

Example **Would** you like some coffee?
You **should** study hard to pass the test.
Could you open the window?
Can you speak Korean?
I **might** see you later.
You **must** have a visa to visit Australia.
Will you finish this work for me?

To make a modal verb negative you should use "not" after the modal verb.

Example He **should** not smoke in the office.
They **might** not come to the meeting.

Section 3 Conversation 1 – Shopping

① Try the following conversation with your partner.

Saleswoman	Can I help you?
Customer	Yes. I'd like to buy these 2 pairs of shoes please. How much are they?
Saleswoman	They are regularly $19.99. But today we are having a 2 for 1 sale. So your total for both will come to $19.99 plus tax. How would you like to pay for them?
Customer	I'll pay for them with my credit card.
Saleswoman	Ok. Here is your receipt. Thank you and have a nice day.
Customer	You're welcome.

Saleswoman	도와드릴까요?
Customer	예, 이들 신발 2켤레를 구매하고 싶습니다. 얼마입니까?
Saleswoman	정가로 19불 99센트입니다만, 오늘은 1회에 2켤레를 팔고 있습니다. 그래서 둘 다 모두 합쳐서 세금 포함 19불 99센트가 되겠습니다. 어떻게 지불하시겠습니까?
Customer	신용카드로 지급하겠습니다.
Saleswoman	좋습니다. 영수증 여기 있습니다. 감사합니다. 좋은 하루 되세요.
Customer	천만에요. 감사합니다.

Section 4 Exercise 1

Make a team of three or four people. Pick something from your bag and try and practice selling it to your teammates. Take turns being the buyer and seller.

Section 5 Conversation 2 – Exchanging an Item

① Try the following conversation with your partner.

Customer	I'd like to return this sweater. It's too small for my brother. Could I exchange it for a bigger one?
Salesperson	I'll check the computer and see if we have a larger one. But I think we might have sold the last one yesterday.
Customer	Thank you for checking.
Salesperson	I'm sorry, but we are sold out of that item.
Customer	Can I get a refund?
Salesperson	I will need to see your receipt.
Customer	Here it is.
Salesperson	Just a moment please. I will get your refund.

Customer	이 스웨터를 물리고 싶은데요. 내 동생에게 너무 작아요. 더 큰 것으로 바꿀 수 있나요?
Salesperson	컴퓨터를 체크해 보고 더 큰 것을 가지고 있는지 보겠습니다. 그러나 어제 마지막 하나를 팔았던 것으로 생각합니다.
Customer	체크해 주셔서 감사해요.
Salesperson	미안합니다. 그 품목이 다 팔렸습니다.
Customer	환불받을 수 있나요?
Salesperson	영수증 보여주세요.
Customer	여기 있습니다.
Salesperson	잠깐만요. 환불해 드리겠습니다.

Exercise 2

① Use the correct modal verbs in the following sentences. There is more than one possible answer for each statement.

could | should | would | can | may | might | must | will

1. He ______________ play the piano and guitar too.
2. Children ______________ not sit too close to the television.
3. Our department ______________ have the report ready by tomorrow or the boss will be angry.
4. You ______________ be able to fly to New York on Monday, but we are not sure yet because of the bad weather.
5. I ______________ like the steak and rice please.

② Make a team of 3 people. Ask and answer the following questions.

1. Where is your favorite place to go shopping?
2. Which stores often have a buy 1 get 1 free sale?
3. What item is usually sold out when you go shopping?
4. Which things have a high tax on them?
5. Can you name a business that gives good discounts?
6. What is more important to you, price or brand name?

Section 7 **Reading**

1 Reading Ads

2 Read the following ad and answer the questions below.

Greg Brown Construction LTD.

For All Your New Home Construction & General Contracting Needs

No Job Too Big or Too Small

Renovations & Additions–Decks–Roofing–Windows–Garage Packages–Concrete Work

ALL WORK GUARANTEED–FREE ESTIMATES

Ph: 541–1851 bossyboss@gbc.com

3 Are these statements True (T) or False (F)?

1. ______________ They can fix the roof on your house.
2. ______________ The company only does small construction jobs.
3. ______________ The company does not guarantee their work.
4. ______________ You can learn the cost of your project for free.
5. ______________ They can build many different types of garages.
6. ______________ You cannot contact them through the Internet.

Section 8 Speaking

1 Ask and answer the following questions.

1. What is something you want to buy?
2. How much will it cost?
3. Where is a good place to buy it?
4. Have you ever sold something? What was it?
5. Do you think you would like a job meeting customers?

Section 9 Review

1 Find the mistake(s) and rewrite the sentences.

1. The warranty has expiry on that item.

____

2. The television comes to $450 plus sales taxi.

____

3. I heard that the department store is having a going into business sale.

____

4. I'm sorry sir but we are selled out of that item.

____

5. I want to be there early because the 1 for 2 sale starts tomorrow.

____

Section 10 Shopping Online

① Try the following conversation with your partner.

Austin	Yerin, I see you like shopping on that website a lot. Why do you like it so much?
Yerin	Well, first of all they offer free shipping. Also this site allows customers to divide their payments over 3 months.
Austin	That sounds great. I didn't know people could do that. So are there any benefits if I spend a lot of money on that site?
Yerin	Oh yes! If you spend more than 50,000 won there is no interest on the payments. If you spend more than 100,000 won they will send you a 10% discount coupon. You can use it next time you shop on their site.
Austin	That is amazing. I'm going to check it out. What is the name of that website again?
Yerin	It's www.onlinsuperstore.co.kr. If you need any help searching for something let me know.

Austin	예린, 내가 보기에 당신은 그 웹사이트 쇼핑을 매우 좋아하는가 봐. 왜 그렇게 많이 좋아하나요?
Yerin	음, 무엇보다도 무료배송을 지원하거든요. 또한 본 사이트에서는 고객들에게 3개월에 걸쳐 할부 결재가 허용되어요.
Austin	그거 참 좋은데요. 나는 사람들이 그걸 할 수 있는지 몰랐네요. 그래서 내가 만약 그 사이트에 많은 돈을 지출하면 어떤 이익이 있나요?
Yerin	오 그래요! 만약 당신이 50,000원 이상 지출하면 지급액에 대한 이자가 없어요. 만약 100,000원 이상 지출하면 10% 할인쿠폰을 제공할 거예요. 그 사이트에서 다음에 쇼핑할 때 그것을 사용할 수 있어요.
Austin	놀랍군요. 확인해 봐야 겠어요. 그 웹사이트명이 무엇인가요?
Yerin	웹사이트 명은 www.onlinsuperstore.co.kr 입니다. 무엇인가를 찾는데 어떤 도움이 필요하면 알려 주세요.

2 Work together with 3 other students. Ask and answer the following questions.

What kind of:	Student 1	Student 2	Student 3
smartphone would you like to buy?			
clothes would you like to buy?			
drinks do you often buy?			
pizza do you like to buy?			
car would you like to buy?			

3 Ask your partner the following online shopping questions.

1. Do you like shopping online?

___

2. What do you think is the best Korean shopping website?

___

3. What foreign shopping website is popular in Korea?

___

4. What do you like to buy online?

___

5. What is something you would not buy online?

___

6. What kind of food do Koreans like to order online?

___

Telephone & Email

Section 1 Vocabulary

- **answer the phone**
  전화를 받다
- **area code**
  n. (전화의) 지역번호, 시외 국번
- **attachments**
  n. 부착, 부속물, 부착물, 첨부물(파일)
- **call back later**
  나중에 다시 전화 걸다
- **cell phone/mobile phone**
  이동전화, 휴대전화, 핸드폰
- **collect call**
  n. 수신전화
- **connect you**
  너와 연결하다
- **country code**
  n. 국가번호
- **domain name**
  n. 도메인 이름
- **email**
  n. (컴퓨터) 이메일, 전자우편
- **extension**
  n. (선로 · 전화의) 연장선, 내선, 구내전화
- **forward**
  ad. 앞으로, 앞쪽(전방)으로
  a. 앞쪽(전방)으로의, 전진하는, 가는, 앞쪽의
  vt. 전송하다, 회송하다, 발송하다
- **have a nice day**
  즐거운 하루 되세요
- **international call**
  n. 국제전화
- **leave a message**
  메시지를 남기다
- **long distance call**
  n. 장거리 (전화) 통화
- **make a call**
  전화를 걸다
- **put you through**
  연결해 주다
- **receive**
  vt. vi. (제공 · 배달된 것 등을) 받다, 수취하다, 얻다(from)
- **ring**
  n. 벨소리
- **send**
  vt. 1. (명령 · 의뢰 등에 의해서) (사람을) 가게 하다, 파견하다
  2. (물건 등을) 보내다, 부치다, 발송하다, 송달하다

vi. 1. 사람을 보내다, 심부름꾼을 보내다

2. 편지를 보내다, 알리다

- snail mail

n. (email에 비해 도착하는 데 시간이 걸리는) 기존의 보통우편

- take a message

메시지를 받다

- text message

n. (휴대전화) 문자

- unlisted number

n. 기록되어 있지 않은 전화번호

- wrong number

n. 틀린 전화번호

1 Saying Phone Numbers

432–8790 : four three two eight seven nine zero

432–8790 : four three two eight seven nine oh

432–8790 : four three two eighty–seven ninety

Ext. 236 : extension two three six

Ext. 236 : extension two thirty–six

2 International Numbers

1–902–765–9843 : In this telephone number there are three parts.

Country code : 1

Area code : 902

Local number : 765–9843

3 Cell Phone Numbers

Cell Phone numbers often have three digits at the beginning and can include zero as the first number.

010–6875–2489 : oh one oh six eight seven five twenty–four eighty–nine
010–6875–2489 : zero one zero six eight seven five two four eight nine

Section 2 Practice these telephone expressions.

Greetings

Hello. May I speak to Su Jin?
Hello. Is Jin Hee there?
Hello. Can I speak with Michael?
Hello. Could I speak to Mr. Jones please?
Hello. Is Jason around?

Answers

This is Mr. Jones.
This is she/he.
Hold on please.
Just a minute, please.
Just a moment, please.
Sorry. She/he isn't here right now.
Sorry. Su Jin is busy right now.

Messages

Would you like to leave a message?
May I take a message?
Can I leave a message?
Could you take a message for me?
Tell Su Jin to call Brian.
Ask Mr. Jones to call Catherine.
Tell Mr. Jones I will call him later.
Tell Virginia to meet Joe at 3:00 pm.

Section 3 Conversation 1 – Taking a Message

① Try the following conversation with your partner.

Receptionist	Good afternoon. Travel Systems. How can I help you?
Caller	Hi, I'd like to speak to Mrs. Shin, please.
Receptionist	I'm afraid Mrs. Shin isn't in right now. Would you like to leave a message?
Caller	Yes, please tell her that William Smith can't come to the meeting at 3pm tomorrow.
Receptionist	Let me check the message. Your name is William Smith, and you can't come to the meeting at 3pm tomorrow.
Caller	That's right. Thanks for your help.
Receptionist	It's no trouble, sir. Would there be anything else?
Caller	No. That's everything.
Receptionist	Goodbye, sir. Have a nice day.

Receptionist	안녕하세요. 트래벌 시스템입니다. 뭘 도와드릴까요?
Caller	안녕하세요. 미시즈 신과 통화 좀 하고 싶은데요.
Receptionist	미시즈 신은 지금 부재중입니다. 메시지를 남겨주시겠습니까?
Caller	예. 그녀에게 윌리암 스미스는 내일 3시 미팅에는 올 수 없다고 전해 주시기 바랍니다.

Receptionist	메시지를 체크해 보겠습니다. 당신의 이름은 윌리암 스미스, 그리고 내일 3시 미팅에는 올 수 없습니다.
Caller	좋습니다. 도와주셔서 감사합니다.
Receptionist	좋습니다. 그밖에 다른 것이 있으십니까?
Caller	없습니다. 그것이 모두입니다.
Receptionist	안녕히 계십시오. 좋은 하루 되시기 바랍니다.

2 Wrong Numbers

Sometimes a person may call you but ask for a person you don't know. If someone dials the wrong number, you can say:

"Sorry. You have the wrong number."

"There is no one here by that name."

The person will probably say, "I'm sorry" or "I'm sorry about that" and hang up the phone.

Section 4 Exercise

1 Leave messages for the people.

1. A : Hello. May I speak to Hye Won?
   B : I'm sorry. She's not here. May I take a message?
   A : Yes. Tell her to call Brian.

2. A : Hi. Can I speak with June please?
   B : I'm afraid he's not in the office right now. Do you ______________________
   C : Sure. __________________________________

3. A : Hello. Is Jung Hoon around?
   B : He's busy right now. Would __________________________________
   A : Yes I would. Ask Jung Hoon __________________________________

4. A : Hi. Can I speak to David?
   B : Sorry. __________________________________
   A : I'm sorry.

Section 5

Conversation 2 – Forwarding a Call

① Try the following conversation with a partner.

Secretary	Star Electronics. How may I help you?
Mr. Kim	Hello. This is Jung Hoon Kim from the Songdo factory. May I speak to Fred Simpson please?
Secretary	I'm sorry, but Mr. Simpson has gone out to lunch. May I take a message?
Mr. Kim	We have an urgent problem here with the main production line. It's very important that I speak to him now.
Secretary	Okay, Mr. Kim, I will forward your call to Mr. Simpson's cell phone.
Mr. Kim	Thank you very much.

Secretary	Star Electronics. 뭘 도와 드릴까요?
Mr. Kim	안녕하세요. 저는 송도공장의 김정훈이라고 합니다. 프레드 심슨 씨 좀 바꿔주시겠습니까?
Secretary	미안하군요. 심슨 씨는 점심식사하러 나갔습니다. 메시지를 남기시겠어요?
Mr. Kim	여기 주 생산라인에 긴급한 문제가 있어요. 그것은 지금 그에게 말하는 것이 중요합니다.
Secretary	좋아요. 미스터 김. 심슨 씨의 휴대폰으로 전화를 연결해 드리겠습니다.
Mr. Kim	대단히 고맙습니다.

② Talk to a partner and answer the questions.

1. Does Mr. Kim leave a message?
2. Where is the main production line?
3. Where is Mr. Simpson now?
4. Why does Mr. Kim want to speak to Mr. Simpson?
5. How does the secretary contact Mr. Simpson?

Section 6

Conversation 2 – Checking E-mail

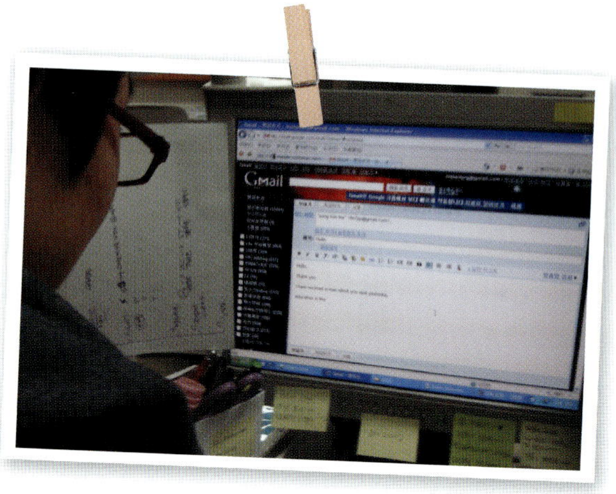

① Try the following conversation with your partner.

Mr. Lee	Have we received an email from Star Electronics yet, Diane?
Diane	Let me check, sir. Ah, yes, it has just arrived.
Mr. Lee	Please forward it to my personal account.
Diane	Yes, sir. Just a moment... there. It's already done.
Mr. Lee	Excellent. Oh, and don't forget to send a Christmas email to all our clients.
Diane	I've just finished doing that this morning, sir.
Mr. Lee	Very good.

Mr. Lee	Star Electronics로부터 이메일을 이미 받았나요, Diane?
Diane	체크해 보겠습니다. 아, 예, 방금 도착했습니다.
Mr. Lee	내 개인 계정으로 전달해 주세요.
Diane	예, 잠깐만요. 지금 막 보냈습니다.
Mr. Lee	잘했어요. 그리고 모든 우리 고객들에게 크리스마스 이메일을 발송하는 것을 잊지 마세요.
Diane	오늘 아침에 그 일 하는 것을 마쳤습니다.
Mr. Lee	아주 좋아요.

2 Formal vs. Informal email

A **Email used in business should have a formal style. The letter should quickly explain what you are writing about.**

Example I am writing to ask about the recent shipment from your factory.

Email used to write friends and family usually has an informal style.

Example Hi, how's it going? I've got some great news.

B **Saying an email address.**

@ : at
. : dot

Example sheila24@earthlink.net : sheila twenty–four at earthlink dot net
monsterjoe@heatmail.com : monster joe at heatmail dot com

Section 7 Email Example

Dear Mr. Park,

I am writing to you to learn more about you XYZ memory chips that have recently been put on sale. Our company is expanding production now and we would like to purchase 30000 chips from your company. Could you please give us a price on the items and a general idea of how long it would take you to ship the items to our factory in Busan.

Thank you for your attention to this matter. We look forward to hearing from you soon.

Sincerely,

Keun Hyoung Lee

Purchasing Manager,
Dongyang Technologies Inc.

A **Email Rules** : Here are some rules to use when writing emails for business.

1. Write in formal style. Use proper grammar and punctuation.

2. Never use ALL CAPS. This is known as "shouting" in email language and it is not professional.

3. Communicate your message quickly and clearly.

4. Make sure you include a greeting and a closing.

5. Attach files in easier to read formats such as MS-Word.

Section 8 Writing an email to your teacher.

① Topic–Missing Class

You missed last week's class. Write an email and give a reason why you missed class. Also, ask what the class studied and ask if there is any homework. This should be a formal email.

Dear ______________________,

____

____

____

____

____

Sincerely,

____

Section 9 Write a Business Email

You are the purchasing manager of Bossy Boss Construction. Your boss wants you to write an email to Chris Taylor, the sales manager at the XYZ Power Tool Company. The boss wants you to order 52 electric power saws and 28 concrete drills from his company.

Ask about : 1. the price. 2. the shipping costs. 3. how long it will take to deliver the items.

____

___________________________,

History of the Telephone

Alexander Graham Bell invented the telephone in 1876 in the United States. The first telephones were very simple. A caller called a switchboard, which then connected the caller to the person they wanted to speak to. Now we can call someone directly. Bell Labs made the first cell phone in 1947. However, its batteries were too big for practical use. Then in the 1970s Motorola made cell phones for commercial sale. The first cell phones could only make calls. Now cell phones can send text messages, email, use the Internet, play songs and receive TV shows. By 1985, there were about 300,000 cell phones in America and only 900 cell phone towers. Now there are over 200 million cell phone users in America and over 200,000 cell phone towers. China has the most cell phone users in the world, with more than 400 million.

전화의 역사

알렉산더 그래햄 벨은 1876년 미국에서 전화를 발명했다. 그 당시의 첫 전화는 매우 단순했다. 전화를 거는 사람이 교환대에 전화하고, 그러면 교환대는 전화를 거는 사람을 통화를 하고 싶은 사람에게 연결시켜 주었다. 지금은 어떤 사람에게 직접 전화를 할 수 있다. 벨 실험실은 1947년에 첫 휴대폰을 만들었다. 그러나, 배터리는 실용적으로 사용하기에는 너무 컸다. 그래서 1970년대 모토로라는 상업적인 판매를 위해 휴대폰을 만들었다. 첫 휴대폰은 단지 전화만 할 수 있었다. 지금은 휴대폰을 통해 문자 메시지, 이메일 보내기 및 인터넷 이용을 할 수 있고 그리고 노래연주와 TV쇼를 수신할 수도 있다. 1985년까지, 미국에 약 300,000개의 휴대폰과 단지 900개의 휴대폰 탑이 있었다. 지금은 미국에 2억 개 이상의 휴대폰과 200,000개의 휴대폰 탑이 있다. 중국은 4억 개 이상의 휴대폰을 보유함으로써 세계에서 가장 많은 휴대폰 이용자들을 가지고 있다.

① Talk to a partner and answer the questions.

1. Who invented the telephone? When and where did he invent it?
2. When was the first cell phone invented?
3. Why was the first cell phone difficult to use?
4. What company made the first practical cell phones?
5. Could the first cell phones send text messages?
6. How many cell phones and cell towers are in America now?
7. Which country has the most cell phone users? How many cell phone users does it have?

Trade

Section 1 Vocabulary

- availability
  n. 유효성, 유용성, 효용, (입수)가능성
- balance of payments
  n. (국제)수지
- cash on delivery(COD)
  n. 대금 상환 인도
- complaint
  n. 불만, 불평
- delayed
  늦춰진, 미뤄진
- demand
  vt. 요구(요청)하다(ask for), 필요로 하다
  n. 요구, 수요, 청구
- export
  vt. vi. 수출하다
  n. 수출
- import
  vt. (상품을) 수입하다
  vi. 중요하다, 중대한 관계가 있다
  n. 수입
- letter of credit
  n. 신용장(L/C)
- price
  n. 값, 가격, 대가, 정가, 시세, 시가
- satisfactory/satisfied
  n. 선적(船積), 수송, 발송, 출하
- shipment
  adj. 만족스러운
- supply
  vt. (필요품 등을) 공급하다, 주다
  vi. 대리를 맡아보다, 대리하다
  n. (수요에 대한) 공급
- trading
  상업에 종사하는, 통상용의
- trading partner
  n. 무역 상대국
- wire transfer
  n. 전신 송금

Section 2-1

Grammar

① Complaints

A complaint is made when you are not satisfied with a product or service.

② Ways to complain

The service is not satisfactory.

I want to make a complaint.

I don't like this.

I think there is a problem.

I'd hate to complain, but ______________.

③ Ways to respond

I'm sorry. What seems to be the problem?

I'll take care of that right away.

We'll change that immediately.

I promise it won't happen again.

I'll look into it as soon as possible.

Section 2-2 Complaining Politely

① When you complain or talk about a problem you can be more polite if you use **not very** and an opposite adjective.

The sweater is ugly. The sweater **isn't very** pretty.

The new items are dirty. The new items are **not very** clean.

② Rewrite these sentences using **not very**.

1. The hotel room is dirty.

____

2. The delivery company is slow.

____

3. The software is useless.

____

4. He is lazy.

____

5. The price is a rip off.

____

Section 3 Conversation 1 – Delayed Shipment

① Try the following conversation with your partner.

Mr. Davis	Joe, has the shipment been sent to Korea yet?
Joe	No, Mr. Davis, it's going to be sent tomorrow.
Mr. Davis	That is not satisfactory. What happened?
Joe	I'm sorry, but we had some problems and we had to delay the final shipping date.
Mr. Davis	That's the third time you have delayed our shipments. I think we are going to change shippers in the future.
Joe	I promise it won't happen again. Please give us another chance.
Mr. Davis	No, I'm sorry, but my company cannot afford anymore of your mistakes.
Joe	I'm sorry to hear that.

Mr. Davis	Joe, 선적품이 한국으로 이미 발송되었나요?
Joe	아닙니다, 미스터 데이비스, 내일 발송될 예정입니다.
Mr. Davis	만족스럽지 않군요. 무슨 일이지요?
Joe	미안합니다만, 약간의 문제가 있어서 마지막 선적일을 연기해야만 했습니다.
Mr. Davis	우리 선적품을 연기한 것이 세 번째입니다. 앞으로 화주를 바꿔야겠다는 생각을 하고 있습니다.
Joe	다시는 이런 일이 없도록 하겠습니다. 다른 기회를 좀 주시기 바랍니다.
Mr. Davis	아니요, 미안합니다만, 더 이상의 당신의 실수를 참을 수가 없습니다.
Joe	그런 말씀을 듣게 되어 유감이군요.

Section 4 Exercise 1

① Talk to another student and use the information below to make complaints.

1. You have to pay more money than you planned.
2. Your coworker is not working hard.
3. The internet has stopped working
4. A customer is late paying your company.
5. You receive damaged items from a delivery person.

Section 5 Conversation 2 – Placing an Order

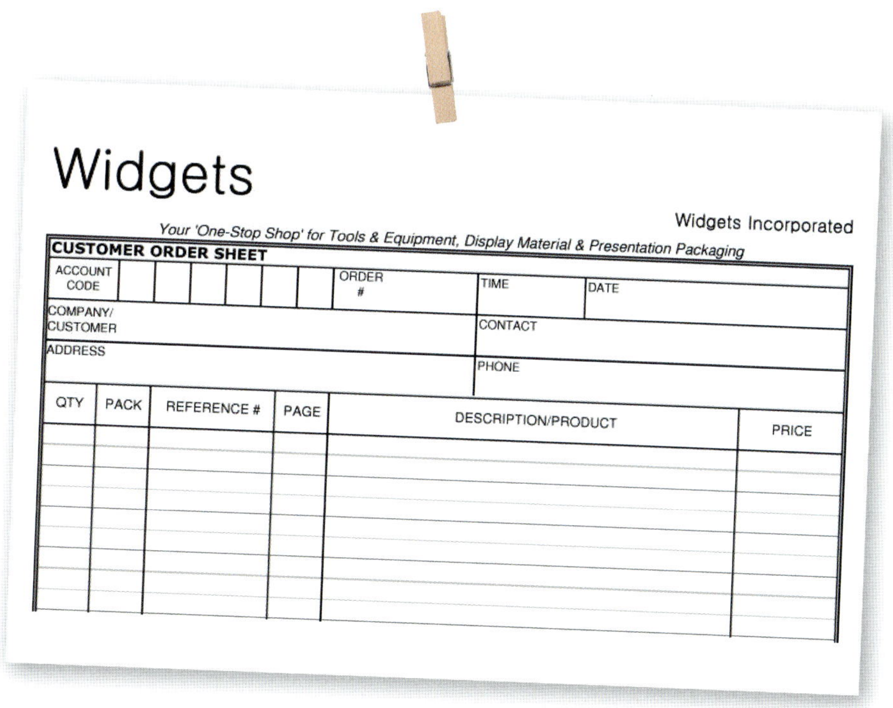

Widgets

Widgets Incorporated

Your 'One-Stop Shop' for Tools & Equipment, Display Material & Presentation Packaging

CUSTOMER ORDER SHEET

ACCOUNT CODE		ORDER #		TIME		DATE	
COMPANY/ CUSTOMER				CONTACT			
ADDRESS				PHONE			

QTY	PACK	REFERENCE #	PAGE	DESCRIPTION/PRODUCT	PRICE

① Try the following conversation with your partner.

Supplier	Good morning, Widgets Incorporated. How may I help you?
Customer	Yes, I would like to order **500** widgets, please.
Supplier	Okay. What's the destination?
Customer	**San Francisco, USA.**
Supplier	Alright, your shipment will arrive in **three days**. The cost is one dollar per widget plus **$100** for shipping. How would you like to pay?
Customer	**Letter of credit.**
Supplier	Fine. So that comes to **$600**. Please call if there are any problems with the shipment.
Customer	Thank you.

Supplier	안녕하세요? Widgets사입니다. 뭘 도와드릴까요?
Customer	예, 500개의 위젯을 주문하고 싶습니다.
Supplier	좋습니다. 목적지가 어디세요?
Customer	미국 San Francisco입니다.
Supplier	좋아요. 선적품은 3일 내에 도착할 것입니다. 비용은 선적비 100불을 포함하여 위젯당 1달러입니다. 대금결제는 어떻게 하시겠습니까?
Customer	신용장결제방식으로 하겠습니다.
Supplier	좋아요. 600불이 됩니다. 만약 선적품에 문제가 있으면 연락주세요.
Customer	감사합니다.

Section 6 Exercise 2

Practice the conversation in Section 5. Replace the information in **BOLD** letters. Take turns being the Supplier and Customer.

1. Amount of Widgets : **1000** Destination : **San Paulo, Brazil** Shipping Time/Cost : **two weeks/$300** Payment : **Wire transfer.** Total Amount : **$1300**	2. Amount of Widgets : **750** Destination : **Moscow, Russia.** Shipping Time/Cost : **one week/$250** Payment : **Half now, half on delivery, by wire transfer** Total Amount : **$1000**
3. Amount of Widgets : **4000** Destination : **Sydney, Australia** Shipping Time/Cost : **Three weeks/$500** Payment Method : **Letter of Credit** Total Amount : **$4500**	4. Amount of Widgets : **2500** Destination : **Toronto, Canada** Shipping Time/Cost : **1 day/$50** Payment Method : **COD Total** Amount : **$2550**

Section 7 **Reading**

International Trade

International trade consists of exports and imports. Exports are things a country sells to other countries. Imports are things a country buys from other countries. For example, Korea exports cars and imports oil. The difference between exports and imports is called the balance of payments. To have a strong economy a country wants to export more than it imports. This means it has a positive balance of payments. Trade depends on many factors. Quality of products is important, as well as price and availability. The biggest factor in trade is supply and demand. Customers demand a certain product and suppliers supply it. Sometimes demand is less and suppliers can't sell their products. Then they must stockpile it and hope demand is going to rise in the future. If demand doesn't rise or is less, then a supplier may be forced out of business because no one wants their products.

국제무역

국제무역은 수출과 수입으로 이루어진다. 수출품은 일국에서 다른 나라로 파는 것들이다. 수입품은 일국이 다른 나라들로부터 사는 것들이다. 예컨대, 한국은 자동차를 수출하고 오일을 수입한다. 수출과 수입 간의 차액을 국제수지라 부른다. 강한 경제를 갖기 위해 일국은 수입보다는 수출을 더 원한다. 이것은 양의 국제수지를 갖는다는 걸 의미한다. 무역은 많은 요소에 의존하고 있다. 제품의 품질은 가격 및 입수가능성과 마찬가지로 중요하다. 무역에서 가장 중요한 것은 공급과 수요이다. 고객은 어떤 제품을 요구하고 공급자들은 제품을 공급한다. 때때로 수요가 더 적어서 공급자들은 그들의 제품을 판매할 수가 없게 된다.그러면 그들은 제품을 비축할 수밖에 없게 된다. 그래서 앞으로 수요가 올라가기를 희망한다. 만약 수요가 올라가지 않거나 더 적다면 공급자는 어쩔 수 없이 파산할지도 모른다. 왜냐하면 아무도 그들의 제품을 원하지 않기 때문이다.

1 Are these statements True (T) or False (F)?

1. Exports are things you buy from other countries. ______________

2. One of Korea's exports are cars. ______________

3. Trade depends only on quality of a product. ______________

4. Products are demanded by customers. ______________

5. If demand is less, products can't be sold. ______________

6. Suppliers give away products they can't sell. ______________

Section 8 Review

① Find the mistakes and rewrite the sentences

1. I want order 10,000 widgets.

2. How would you like to paid?

3. The ship time is two weeks.

4. Imports are things you by from other countries.

5. I want to complaining about the noise.

6. I sorry. It won't happen again. I promise.

7. Please don't give me another chance.

8. I'm sorry, but your work is satisfactory.

Section 9 Speaking

① Ask and answer the following questions with your partner.

1. Which countries does Korea export a lot of things to?
2. Which countries does Korea import a lot of things from?
3. Is complaining on the internet a good way to complain?
4. What kind of items does Korea export a lot of?
5. What kind of items does Korea import a lot of?

Section 10 Conversation 3 – Shipping Items

① Try the following conversation with your partner.

Ashley	Excuse me Brandon. I have just received an email from our customer in France. They are asking if it is possible to send their shipment by sea.
Brandon	When do they want the items?
Ashley	They say they want to receive the items by the 23rd of this month.
Brandon	That is 2 weeks from now. There is no way we can deliver the items that quickly by sea. Tell them air shipment is the only way we can deliver the items by the 23rd.
Ashley	They said air shipment is too expensive. They want to keep costs down.
Brandon	Send them an email. Tell them if they want it fast, they have to pay more.
Ashley	Okay. I'll tell them right away.

Ashley	실례해요. 브랜던. 프랑스 고객으로부터 방금 이메일을 받았어요. 선편으로 화물발송이 가능한지 질문을 하더군요.
Brandon	그 물품을 원하는 때는 언제인가요?
Ashley	이 달 23일까지 그 물품을 수령하기를 원한다고 합니다.
Brandon	지금부터 2주일이군요. 선편으로 그렇게 빨리 물품을 인도할 수 있는 방법은 없습니다. 항공운송만이 23일까지 그 물품을 인도할 수 있는 유일한 방법이라고 말해 주세요.
Ashley	항공운송은 너무 비싸다고 하더군요. 그들은 비용절감을 원해요.
Brandon	이메일을 보내주세요. 빠른 것을 원한다면, 더 많이 지불해야 한다고 하세요.
Ashley	좋아요. 즉시 말할께요.

② Ask your partner about the details in the previous conversation.

1. Where is the shipment being sent?

2. When does the French company want the shipment?

3. Why does the French company want shipment by sea?

4. What is the problem with shipping the items by sea?

5. What is the advantage of air shipment?

6. What is the disadvantage of air shipment?

7. What does Brandon tell Ashley to say in the email?

UNIT 9

Meetings

Section 1 Vocabulary

- after
  1. (차례) 뒤에
  2. (때) 뒤에, 나중에
- afternoon
  n. 오후
- AM
  오전의
- appointment
  n. (만남) 약속, 예약
- around/about
  주위에, 사방에, 둘레에/(관계 · 종사)
  a. …에 관하여(관한), …에 대하여(대한)
- before
  전에, 이전에, 일찍이, 이미
- during
  (특정 기간의) …동안(내내)
- evening
  n. 저녁(때), 밤
- from 9:00 am to 1:00 pm
  오전 9시부터 오후 1시까지
- meet at
  ~을 만나다
- morning
  n. 아침, 오전
- night
  n. 밤, 야간, 저녁
- office hours
  n. 집무(근무)시간, 영업시간
- PM
  오후의
- reschedule
  (행사 · 계획 등의) 예정을 다시 세우다
- schedule
  n. 예정(표), 계획, 스케줄, 일정, 기일
  vt. 예정에 넣다, …의 표(일람표, 목록, 명세서, 시간표)를 작성하다

Section 2 Grammar

1 Prepositions of Time

The words : **in**, **at** and **on** are called prepositions of time. You must use these when you speak about time.

The preposition **in** usually comes before a set period of time.

Example I will meet you **in three hours**.

Example I started working for the company **in 2008**.

The preposition **at** comes before an exact time.

Example I will meet you **at 3:00 pm**.

Example I came to work **at 8:00 am**.

The preposition **on** usually comes before a day.

Example I will meet you **on Monday**.

Example I went to L.A. **on June 27th**.

Write the correct time preposition. Use **on**, **in** or **at** to complete the expressions below.

1. ________ September	2. ________ Friday
3. ________ noon	4. ________ 2002
5. ________ my birthday	6. ________ 5 o'clock
7. ________ Monday morning	8. ________ spring
9. ________ December 25th	10. ________ 30 minutes
11. ________ 9:00 am	12. ________ Valentines Day

Section 3 Conversation 1 – Making an Appointment

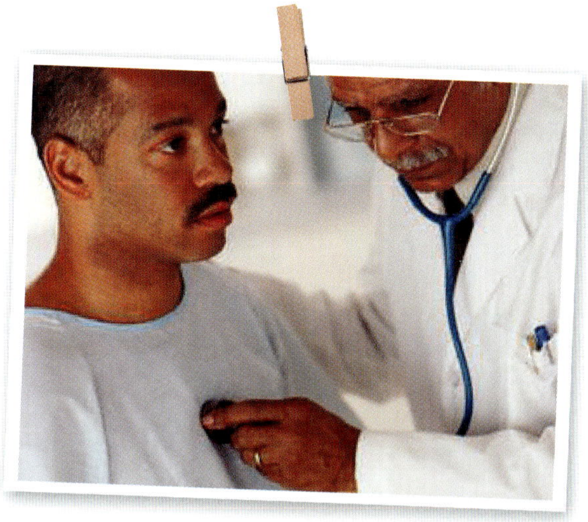

① Try the following conversation with your partner.

George	I'd like to make an appointment to see Dr. Phillips.
Secretary	Sure. Could I have your name please?
George	My name is George O'Neil.
Secretary	What seems to be the problem, Mr. O'Neil?
George	I have a sore back.
Secretary	Can you come in on Tuesday, in the afternoon? The doctor will be in his office at 1:00 pm.
George	Ok, I'll come in at 1:30.
Secretary	Great, we'll see you then.

George	필립스 박사님의 진찰을 받기 위해 약속을 하고 싶습니다.
Secretary	좋아요. 이름을 알려 주세요.
George	조지 오닐입니다.
Secretary	오닐 씨, 무엇이 문제인 것 같습니까?
George	등이 아픕니다.
Secretary	화요일 오후에 오실 수 있어요? 박사님은 오후 1시에 그의 사무실에 오실 겁니다.
George	알았습니다. 1시 30분에 오겠습니다.
Secretary	좋아요, 그때 뵙지요.

Section 4

Exercise 1

① Put the best expression in the blank. Some statements have more than one answer.

about | before | around | during | after | from 3:00 to 5:00 pm

1. The bus leaves at 9:10 am, so make sure you are here ______________ 9:00 am.
2. The meeting will run ______________________________.
3. ______________ take off please keep your seat belts fastened.
4. We are going to arrive late, maybe sometime ______________ 7:30 pm
5. I'm not sure exactly, maybe ______________ 1:00 pm.
6. If you call back ______________ 2:00 pm he should be here.

Section 5

Conversation 2 – Canceling an Appointment

① Try the following conversation with your partner.

Secretary	Good morning, Wilson Hotel Supplies. How may I help you?
Michael	Good morning. I have an appointment to meet the Sales Director tomorrow at 11:30. I'd like to cancel that appointment and reschedule our meeting to next week.
Secretary	The Sales Director is free on Wednesday afternoon. Would 2:30 in the afternoon be ok for you?
Michael	Yes, at 2:30 on Wednesday afternoon would be perfect.
Secretary	May I have your name, sir?
Michael	It's Michael Westin of Holiday Hotels. Thank you for your help.
Secretary	You're welcome, sir.

Secretary	안녕하세요. Wilson Hotel Supplies입니다. 뭘 도와 드릴까요?
Michael	안녕하세요. 내일 11시 30분에 판매이사와 만나기로 약속했습니다. 그 약속을 취소하고 다음 주에 우리 약속을 다시 잡고 싶습니다.
Secretary	판매이사는 수요일 오후에 시간이 있습니다. 오후 2시 30분에 괜찮으신지요?
Michael	예, 수요일 오후 2시 30분에 좋습니다.
Secretary	이름을 좀 알려주시겠어요?
Michael	Holiday Hotels의 마이클 웨스틴입니다. 도와주셔서 감사합니다.
Secretary	천만에요.

Section 6 Making and Canceling an Appointment

① Try making and canceling an appointment with your partner. Take turns being the appointment maker and the secretary.

1. Make an appointment to meet at 9:00 am
2. Make an appointment to visit the manager on Wednesday.
3. Cancel your doctor's appointment on the 23rd.
4. Cancel your airplane reservation to Japan.

Section 7 Reading

Canceling Meetings

Time is very valuable to people. It is very important to cancel a meeting or appointment if you are not going to be there. If you do not cancel, and do not go to the meeting; the people waiting to see you may be angry with you! The person you planned to meet may be only waiting for you, so it is important to not waste people's time. They will be glad that you canceled and it will make it easier to reschedule a new meeting in the future.

It is also not good to cancel at the last minute. Make sure you can be at your appointment. In business it is always best to be there early, or to cancel early.

미팅 취소

시간은 사람들에게 매우 귀중하다. 만약 당신이 거기에 가지 못한다면 미팅이나 혹은 약속을 취소하는 것은 매우 중요하다. 만약 취소하지 않으면, 그리고 미팅에 가지 않으면, 당신을 만나기 위해 기다리고 있는 사람들은 당신에게 화를 낼지도 모른다. 당신이 만나기로 돼 있는 사람은 단지 당신을 기다리고 있을 뿐인지도 모른다. 그래서 사람들의 시간을 낭비시키지 않는 것은 중요하다. 그들은 당신이 취소한 것과 그로 인해 금후 새로운 스케줄을 잡는 것이 더 용이하게 될 것임을 기뻐할 것이다.

마지막 순간에 취소하는 것도 또한 좋지 않다. 약속을 지킬 수 있도록 다짐하라. 비즈니스에서는 일찍 도착하거나, 혹은 일찍 취소하는

Section 8 **Review**

1 Find the mistake and write the correct sentence.

1. I will see you next Tuesday on 9:30 am.

____

2. The meeting is scheduled to be at March 12th.

____

3. The seminar will be scheduled to March 15th.

____

4. Make sure you give a copy of the plan to the team members during we start the meeting.

____

5. I expect business to turn around on the summer.

____

Section 9 Conversation – Planning a Meeting

① Try the following conversation with your partner.

Secretary	You wanted to see me Mrs. Johnson?
Mrs. Johnson	Yes. We have to plan our monthly sales meeting. What day is best?
Secretary	I think Friday, March 23rd is the best day. Most of the sales people will be in town then.
Mrs. Johnson	Good. Let's have the meeting at 12:00 pm in the main conference room.
Secretary	We should serve some snacks if it is at lunch time.
Mrs. Johnson	Okay. Order some sandwiches and make sure we have plenty of coffee and other drinks.
Secretary	I'll take care of it today.
Secretary	Mrs. Johnson 나를 만나자고 했어요?
Mrs. Johnson	그래요. 월례 세일즈미팅 계획을 세워야 해요. 언제가 가장 좋을까요?
Secretary	3월 23일 금요일이 가장 좋은 날이라고 생각해요. 대부분의 판매원들은 그때 도시에 올거예요.
Mrs. Johnson	좋아요. 주회의실에서 12시에 미팅을 갖도록 해요.
Secretary	점심시간이라면 약간의 스낵을 내놓아야 겠군요.
Mrs. Johnson	그래요. 약간의 샌드위치를 주문하고 그리고 충분한 커피와 다른 음료수를 꼭 준비하도록 하세요.
Secretary	오늘 처리하도록 할게요.

2 Ask your partner about the details in the previous conversation.

1. What kind of meeting are they planning?

2. What day and date will the meeting be held?

3. What time is the meeting?

4. Where will the meeting be held?

5. What will they serve to eat and drink at the meeting?

6. When will the secretary make arrangements for the meeting?

7. Why does the secretary think the 23rd is a good day for the meeting?

Section 10 A Busy Week

① Look at David's calendar for next week.

Day and Date	Schedule
Monday April 10	12:00 PM – lunch with client 3:00 PM – sales meeting
Tuesday April 11	7:15 AM – play squash with Joe 7:00 PM – dinner with Taylor
Wednesday April 12	9:30 AM – meeting with boss 4:00 PM – dentist appointment
Thursday April 13	2:45 PM – sales meeting 8:30 PM – movie with Taylor
Friday April 14	10:00 AM – go to airport. 12:15 PM – fly to LA sales convention
Saturday April 15	All day at sales convention.
Sunday April 16	5:30 PM – fly back home

2 Write an answer to each question and then talk to a partner.

1. What day and time does David fly to LA? How long will he be there?

2. Why is David going to LA?

3. How often will David meet Taylor this week? What will they do?

4. What days and times does David have sales meetings next week?

5. What will David do on the morning of April 11?

6. What day and time will he have a dentist appointment?

7. When is David meeting his boss?

8. Who will David have lunch with on Monday April 10?

UNIT 10 Travel

Section 1 Vocabulary

- **airport tax**
  n. 항공 세금
- **arrival**
  n. 도착
- **Baggage Claim**
  공항의 수화물 찾는 곳
- **brochure**
  n. (업무 안내 등의) 팸플릿, 가제본 한 책, 소책자
- **carry-on bag**
  n. 비행기 안에 가지고 들어갈 수 있는 가방
- **check in/out(hotel)**
  (호텔에서의) 숙박 수속을 하다/(계산을 치르고) 호텔에서 나오다
- **Check In(airport)**
  공항에서의 탑승수속
- **checked baggage**
  n. 승인된 수화물
- **connecting flight**
  비행기를 갈아타다
- **Customs(Form)**
  n. 세관신고서
- **Declare**
  vt. 1. 선언(포고)하다, 공표하다, 선고하다
  2. (세관에서) 신고하다
- **Departure**
  n. 출발, 발차
- **Duty Free**
  a. ad. 관세가 없는(없이), 면세의(로)
  n. 면세품
- **Flight Number**
  n. (정기항공) 편 번호
- **final boarding call**
  최종탑승 벨소리
- **general boarding call**
  일반탑승 벨소리
- **hotel**
  n. 호텔
  vt. (hotelled; hotelling) 호텔(여관)에 묵게 하다

- Immigration(Form)

n. 입국신고서

- lavatory

n. (비행기내) 화장실

- motel

n. 모텔

vi. 모텔에 숙박하다

- No Smoking

금연

- Nothing to Declare

신고할 것이 없는

- occupied

사용중(화장실 따위의 게시)

- Passport Number

n. 여권번호

- pre-boarding call

우선탑승 벨소리

- reservation

n. (방 · 좌석 등의) 예약, 지정

- Security

n. 안전, 무사, 보증

- vacant

a. 빈, 공허한, 빈자리의

- Visa

n. 사증, 비자, 입국 허가

Section 2 Grammar

When you travel it is important to plan for the future. When talking about the future you will use two common expressions, **will** and **going to**. Both of these expressions have basically the same meaning. You need to use them when you speak about the future. Practice saying the examples below.

1 The future with **will + verb**

- stay – will stay
- have – will have
- make – will make
- take – will take
- work – will work
- speak – will speak
- visit – will visit
- call – will call

2 The future with **going to + verb**

- stay – going to stay
- have – going to have
- make – going to make
- take – going to take
- work – going to work
- speak – going to speak
- visit – going to visit
- call – going to call

Section 3 Conversation 1 – Immigration

① Try the following conversation with your partner.

Official	May I see your passport, please?
Jung Min	Yes, sir. Here it is.
Official	How long will you stay in the country?
Jung Min	I'll be here for three days. Then I'm going to fly back to Korea.
Official	What is the purpose of your visit?
Jung Min	I'm here on business.
Official	Ok, enjoy your stay here.
Jung Min	Thank you, sir.

Official	여권 좀 보여 주시겠어요?
Jung Min	예. 여기 있습니다.
Official	얼마 동안 머무르시겠습니까?
Jung Min	이곳에서 3일 동안 있을 겁니다. 그리고 나서 한국으로 되돌아갈 예정입니다.
Official	방문 목적은 무엇입니까?
Jung Min	사업상 이곳에 왔습니다.
Official	알았습니다. 이곳에서 즐거운 체류가 되십시오.
Jung Min	감사합니다.

Section 4 Exercise 1

① Look at the completed immigration form.

1. Family Name	K I M
2. First(given) Name	J U N G H O O N
3. Birth Date(Day/Mo/Yr)	0 2 0 1 7 7
4. Country of Citizenship	K O R E A
5. Sex(Male or Female)	M A L E
6. Passport Number	J X 1 2 2 5 7 7 7
7. Airline and Flight Number	K E 0 1 7
8. Country Where You Live	K O R E A
9. City Where You Boarded	I N C H E O N
10. City Where Visa Was Issued	S E O U L
11. Date Issued(Day/Mo/Yr)	0 7 0 7 0 9
12. Address While in the United States(Number and Street)	S T A R D U S T H O T E L
13. City and State	L A S V E G A S N V

- Family Name : Kim
- First Name : Jung Hoon
- Birth Date : 2/01/77(day/month/year)
- Country of Citizenship : KOREA
- Sex(male or female) : MALE
- Passport Number : JX1225777
- Airline and Flight Number : KE 017
- Country Where you Live : KOREA
- City Where you Boarded : INCHEON
- Country Where Visa was Issued : SEOUL
- Date Issued : 7/07/2009(day/month/year)
- Address While in the US : STARDUST HOTEL
- City and State : Las Vegas NV

② Filling out an Immigration Form

Complete the immigration form. Use your own information.

1. Family Name	
2. First(given) Name	3. Birth Date(Day/Mo/Yr)
4. Country of Citizenship	5. Sex(Male or Female)
6. Passport Number	7. Airline and Flight Number
8. Country Where You Live	9. City Where You Boarded
10. City Where Visa Was Issued	11. Date Issued(Day/Mo/Yr)
12. Address While in the United States(Number and Street)	
13. City and State	

Section 5 Conversation 2 – Getting a Hotel Room

① Try the following conversation with your partner.

Harry	I'd like to check into my room please. I have a reservation.
Receptionist	Certainly, sir. Could I have your name please?
Harry	It's Harry Richard.
Receptionist	It says here you are going to stay for three nights. Is that correct?
Harry	Yes, it is. Can you tell me when breakfast is served?
Receptionist	Breakfast is from 6:00 am to 10:00 am. Here is your room key. Your room number is 1242.
Harry	Thank you very much.
Receptionist	You're welcome.

Harry	방을 체크인하고 싶습니다. 예약을 해 두었습니다.
Receptionist	틀림없군요. 이름 좀 알려 주시겠어요?
Harry	해리 리차드입니다.
Receptionist	여기에 당신은 3박 동안 머무는 것으로 돼 있습니다. 맞습니까?
Harry	그렇습니다. 언제 아침식사가 제공되는지 알려 주시겠습니까?
Receptionist	아침은 오전 6시부터 10시까지입니다. 방 키 여기 있습니다. 방 번호는 1242입니다.
Harry	대단히 감사합니다.
Receptionist	천만에요.

Section 6 Exercise 2

1. Read the motel ad below and answer the following questions.

Stardust Motel

1076 Bedford Highway, Bedford, Alberta

WINTER SPECIAL Any Night for $64.95 + tax (with ad)

Includes Full Breakfast Maximum 2 persons per room.

Certain restrictions apply. Expires March 1

TOLL FREE : 1–788–555–3316

1. When does the winter special end?

2. To get the winter special, what do you need to show the receptionist?

3. How many people can stay in a room?

4. How much does the hotel breakfast cost?

5. How can you make a reservation?

Section 7 Reading

Immigration Forms

It is very important that you have your immigration and customs forms completed properly. If there is a mistake it can cause delays for you at immigration and customs when you enter the country. Many Korean travelers confuse first and last name sections on the forms because they are not used to writing their names in a foreign style. Most foreign countries want your birth date written as (day/month/year). Koreans are used to writing dates as (year/month/day). Make sure the information on your immigration and customs forms match the information in your passport.

입국심사 양식

입국심사 및 세관 통관 양식을 정확히 기재하는 것은 매우 중요하다. 만약 실수가 있다면, 입국시에 입국심사와 세관 통관 지연의 원인이 될 수 있다. 많은 한국 여행자들은 양식상의 이름 및 성(姓) 난(欄)을 혼동한다. 왜냐하면 외국 스타일로 이름을 쓰는 데 익숙하지 않기 때문이다. 대부분의 외국 국가들은 일/월/연도로 쓴 출생일을 원한다. 한국인들은 연도/월/일로 출생일을 쓰는 것에 익숙해 있다. 입국심사와 세관통관 양식에 관한 정보는 여권에 있는 정보와 반드시 일치해야 한다.

1 Are these statements True (T) of False (F)?

1. ________ All passengers must fill out a customs and immigration form.
2. ________ There will be no delays if there is a mistake.
3. ________ Korean travelers sometimes confuse first and last name.
4. ________ Overseas your birthday is usually written as day/month/year.
5. ________ The information on your immigration form does not have to be the same as your passport.

Section 8 **Review**

1 Find the mistake and write the correct sentence.

1. We have to hurry because they just made the finish boarding call.

____

2. I'm sorry, miss, I don't have a reserve.

____

3. You are allowed to checked bags and one carry–on bag.

____

4. I am going the hotel after my flight arrives.

____

5. I have to wait for 2 hours before my flight connecting leaves.

____

Section 9

Speaking

1 Ask and answer the following questions with your partner.

1. Do you have a laptop? What kind is it?
2. Do you travel with your laptop?
3. Have you been to another country or some place far away?
4. Did you have a good time?
5. Do you like taking a package tour?
6. What is your favorite way to travel?
7. What do you like to take with you when you travel?

Section 10 Conversation 3 – Airline Check In

① Try the following conversation with your partner.

Airline Worker	Good afternoon, sir. Could I see your ticket and passport please?
Randall	Oh, yes, here they are. Miss is it possible to get an aisle seat?
Airline Worker	Yes, sir, an aisle seat is no problem. Could you please put your checked bag on the scale? I'm sorry, sir, but I see that your bag is 6 kilograms overweight.
Randall	Oh, no. Is that a problem? Do I have to pay extra for that?
Airline Worker	Yes, sir. There will be an extra charge of $50 for the overweight bag. Do you want to pay by cash or credit?
Randall	I'll pay for it by credit card.

Airline Worker	안녕하세요. 티켓과 여권 좀 보여주시겠어요?
Randall	오 그래요. 여기 있어요. 통로쪽 좌석이 가능한가요?
Airline Worker	예, 통로쪽 좌석이 있습니다. 부칠 가방을 저울 위에 올려 주시겠어요? 미안합니다만, 귀하의 백은 6킬로그램 중량초과입니다.
Randall	오 안돼요. 문제가 있어요? 추가로 돈을 지불해야 하나요?
Airline Worker	예. 중량초과 가방에 대해 50불의 추가요금을 내야 합니다. 현금으로 아니면 신용카드로 결재하시겠어요?
Randall	신용카드로 결재하겠습니다.

2 Airline Vocabulary

Put the correct vocabulary word in the blank.

flight number	airport tax	lavatory	customs form	checked baggage
pre boarding call	duty free	departure	security	

1. I'd like to drop by the ______________________ to buy my dad a gift.

2. The ______________________ time for flight 815 has been delayed 30 minutes.

3. For safety reasons you are not permitted to carry liquids, gels or aerosols through ______________________.

4. Excuse me miss. There is no toilet paper in the ______________________.

5. The ______________________ is included in the price of your ticket.

6. The ______________________ is KE072.

7. This is the ______________________ for flight KE072 bound for Atlanta.

8. My ______________________ didn't arrive.

9. Make sure you have your ______________________ ready for entering the United States.

③ Getting a Train Ticket

Complete the conversation with the vocabulary words below. Then practice the conversation together with your partner.

train	seat	platform	rest	any place	throughout	snack	full service
one way	pleasure	leaving	economy	nice	total	take	difference

A : Hello miss, I'd like to buy a ______________ ticket on the next train to Chicago.

B : The next train ______________ for Chicago is at 7:45 pm. Would you prefer economy or first class?

A : What is the price ______________ between the two? And how long will it ______________ to get to Chicago?

B : Economy is $145.75 and first class is $182.50. The ______________ time to Chicago is 4 hours and 35 minutes.

A : I think I'll give first class a try. Maybe I can get some ______________ on the train.

B : Very good sir. The ______________ departs from ______________ number 3 at 7:45 pm. Your ______________ number is B1 and you will be in car number 2.

A : Is there ______________ to eat on the train?

B : Yes sir. Car number 4 is a ______________ dining car and there is a mobile ______________ cart that goes ______________ the train.

A : Thank you very much.

B : My ______________ sir. Have a nice trip.

UNIT 11

In the Hotel

Section 1 Vocabulary

- bus stop
  버스 정류장
- business center
  n. 비즈니스 센터
- brochure
  n. (업무 안내 등의) 팸플릿, 가제본 한 책, 소책자
- car rental
  임대 자동차
- charge it to my room
  요금은 제 방으로 달아 주세요
- concierge
  n. (호텔의) 접수계
- convention room
  n. 회의실
- door man
  n. 도어맨, 현관 안내인
- dress code
  n. 복장 규정
- exercise room
  n. 운동실
- service charge
  n. (호텔 등의) 서비스료
- front desk
  n. (호텔 등의) 프런트, 카운터
- front entrance
  정면의 입구
- ice machine
  n. 제빙기
- internet connection
  n. 인터넷 접속, 연결
- mini bar
  n. (호텔 객실 등의) 주류 상비용 소형 냉장고
- parking lot
  주차장
- pool
  n. (수영용) 풀(=swimming pool)
- power point
  n. 콘센트
- projector
  n. 투사기, 영사기, 계획자
- room service
  n. 룸 서비스
- sauna
  n. 사우나, 목욕탕
- taxi stand
  택시 승차장
- valet parking
  대리 주차

Section 2 Grammar

1 Polite Requests

Look at the requests using "can" and "could."

The expressions **could you** and **can you** are used to ask for something. **Can** is more informal and should be used with people you know well. **Could** is more formal and polite. It is best to use **could** when you speak to people you don't know.

2 Informal

Can you help me?

Can you find the elevator?

Can you get that?

3 Formal

Could you tell me where the business lounge is?

Could you give me a map of the area?

Could you please send two extra towels to room 815?

Section 3 Exercise

① Practice writing formal and informal questions using **can** or **could**.

1. Ask your friend for a pen.

2. Ask a hotel worker to where the restaurant is.

3. Ask your teammate to turn off the television.

4. Ask the concierge where the bus stop is located.

5. Ask the front desk when it's time to check out.

6. Ask your friend to pay for the taxi.

Section 4 **Conversation 1**

① Try this conversation together with your partner.

A Calling the Front Desk

Front Desk	Good morning, Front Desk. How may I help you?
Hye Won	Hello, I'm calling to see if there is an Internet connection for this room.
Front Desk	Yes, there is a plug-in for the Internet in the wall behind the desk.
	If you need to send faxes, or make photo copies, the business center is open 24 hours.
Hye Won	Could you tell me where the business center is?
Front Desk	It's located on the second floor, room 212.
Hye Won	Thank you.
Front Desk	You're welcome.

Front Desk	안녕하세요. 프론트 데스크입니다. 뭘 도와 드릴까요?
Hye Won	안녕하세요. 이 방에 인터넷 연결장치가 있는지 알고 싶어 전화합니다.
Front Desk	예, 책상 뒤 벽에 인터넷용 플러그인이 있습니다.
	팩스를 보낼 일이나 사진 복사가 필요하다면 비즈니스 센터가 24시간 개방돼 있습니다.
Hye Won	비즈니스 센터가 어디에 있는지 알려 주시겠습니까?
Front Desk	2층 212호에 있습니다.
Hye Won	감사합니다.
Front Desk	천만에요.

Section 5 Exercise 1

① Fill in the blanks and complete the conversation. Some words will be used twice.

everything | good | anything | room | fried | large | sour | thank

A Call to Room Service

Room Service : Room service, how may I help you?

Guest : ______________ evening. I'd like to order a ______________ sweet and ______________ pork and 2 shrimp ______________ rice please for ______________ 815.

Room Service : That's a ______________ sweet and ______________ pork, and 2 shrimp ______________ rice. Will there be ______________ else?

Guest : No that is ______________.

Room Service : It will be about 30 minutes.

Guest : Ok, ______________ you.

Section 6 Conversation 2 – Reserving a Convention Room

① Try this conversation together with your partner.

Customer	Excuse me, sir. I'd like to reserve a convention room for about 200 people. Do you have one large enough?
Manager	Yes, we have a 400 person capacity convention room on the second floor. When would you like to reserve it?
Customer	We would like to have the convention from 3:00 pm to 6:00 pm on Saturday the 25th if possible.
Manager	Yes, the convention room is available then.
Customer	Does it have a power point projector and screen?
Manager	Yes, sir it does. What is the name of your company?
Customer	It is the Dongyang Technical Corporation.

Customer	실례합니다. 약 200명을 위한 컨벤션 룸을 예약하고 싶은데요. 충분히 큰 것이 있습니까?
Manager	예, 2층에 400명 수용능력의 컨벤션 룸이 있습니다. 언제 예약하실 겁니까?
Customer	가능하다면 25일 토요일 오후 3시부터 6시까지 컨벤션을 갖고자 합니다.
Manager	예, 컨벤션 룸은 그때 가능합니다.
Customer	파워포인트 프로젝터와 스크린이 있습니까?
Manager	예, 있어요. 회사명이 무엇입니까?
Customer	Dongyang Technical Corporation입니다.

Section 7 Reading

The Hotel Neighborhood

When you travel around the world in business you will stay at many different kinds of hotels. Some hotels have excellent business service. But some hotels don't have a business center or even Internet! The good news is that the businesses around the hotel will probably offer business services the hotel does not. You should be able to find what you need near the hotel. This is common in almost every country in the world because business is international, and business people usually need the same services. There is a very high chance that the shop owners near the hotel can speak English, no matter what country you are in.

호텔 이웃

당신은 사업상 전 세계를 여행할 때 많은 상이한 유형의 호텔에서 머문다. 어떤 호텔은 뛰어난 비즈니스 서비스를 제공한다. 그러나 어떤 호텔들은 비즈니스 센터가 없거나 심지어 인터넷도 할 수 없다. 좋은 소식은 호텔 주변의 가게들은 아마도 호텔이 제공하지 못하는 비즈니스 서비스를 제공해 줄 것이라는 점이다. 호텔 근처에서 당신이 필요로 하는 것을 틀림없이 구할 수 있을 것이다. 이것은 세계의 거의 모든 국가에서 공통이다. 왜냐하면 비즈니스는 국제적이고, 비즈니스를 하는 사람들은 통상 동일한 서비스를 필요로 하기 때문이다. 당신이 어떠한 나라에 있더라도 호텔 근처의 가게 주인들은 영어를 할 수 있는 가능성이 매우 높다.

Section 8

Review

1 Find the mistake and write the correct sentence.

1. The room requested you is not available at that time.

____

2. The business center is near the 5th floor.

____

3. You could show me where the taxi stand is?

____

4. You can give me a ride to the convention center?

____

5. A charge service of 10% will be added to the bill.

____

Section 9

Conversation 3 – Checking Out From the Hotel

1 Try the following conversation together with your partner.

Miss Lee	Hi, I'd like to check out please. My room number was 815. Here are the room keys.
Front Desk	Ok, thank you. Miss Lee your total room charges for the mini bar and room service comes to $182.95.
Miss Lee	Ok, I'll put that on my credit card. Sir, my flight doesn't leave until later this evening. Could you please hold my bags here for a few hours while I have dinner and do a little shopping before I go?
Front Desk	Of course, ma'am. Just bring your bags over to the concierge, and he'll take care of them for you. What time will you return to pick up your luggage?
Miss Lee	My flight leaves at 9:00 pm so I should be back here around 5 o'clock. Thank you for your help.
Front Desk	It's my pleasure, ma'am.

Miss Lee	안녕하세요. 체크아웃하겠습니다. 방 번호는 815이고 방 열쇠는 여기 있어요.
Front Desk	알았어요. 고마워요. 전체 숙박료는 미니 바와 룸 서비스를 포함하여 $182.95입니다.
Miss Lee	좋아요. 그걸 신용카드로 하겠습니다. 나의 비행기는 오늘 저녁 늦게라야 출발해요. 내가 떠나기 전 저녁식사 하고 약간의 쇼핑을 할 동안 몇 시간 동안 내 가방을 이곳에 좀 맡아 주시겠어요?
Front Desk	좋아요, 손님. 관리인에게 백을 건네주세요. 그러면 백을 잘 맡아 줄거예요. 몇 시에 수화물을 찾으러 돌아오나요?
Miss Lee	내 비행기는 오후 9시에 떠나요. 그래서 5시경 이곳에 돌아와야 해요. 도와주셔서 감사해요.
Front Desk	저도 기뻐요, 손님.

② Hotel Vocabulary

A Fill in the blanks with the correct vocabulary words.

concierge	shuttle bus	check in	check out	someone
brochure	small print	mini bar	password	

1. Excuse me miss. Could I have the Wi-Fi ____________________ ?

2. I am going to leave my bags with the concierge after I ____________________.

3. ____________________ time is at 3:00 pm.

4. The drinks in the ____________________ are really expensive.

5. Be sure to read the ____________________ on the bottom of the menu.

6. Pardon me, sir. Do you have a map or travel ____________________ for this area?

7. Could you send ____________________ to check the toilet in my room?

8. If you ask the ____________________, I'm sure he can help you find a Korean restaurant nearby.

9. The next ____________________ for the airport is at 10:30.

UNIT 12 Meeting Clients

Section 1 Vocabulary

- **adjust**
  vt. 조절하다, 조정하다
- **atmosphere**
  n. 1. (the atmosphere) (지구를 둘러싼) 대기, (천체를 둘러싼) 가스체
  2. (sing) 분위기, 환경, 주위의 상황
- **clients**
  n. 1. (변호사 등의) 의뢰인
  2. (상인의) 고객, 단골
- **coming along**
  ~진행되다
- **down the street**
  길을 걷다
- **gentlemen**
  신사
- **join**
  vt. 결합하다, 참가하다
  vi. 연결(결합)되다
- **lobby**
  n. 로비, (현관의) 홀
- **midnight**
  n. 한밤중
- **noon**
  n. 정오, 한낮(midday)
- **neighborhood**
  n. 1. 근처, 인근, 이웃
  2. (집합적) 이웃사람들(neighbors), (어떤 지역의) 주민
- **several**
  a. (두셋은 아니고) 몇몇의,
- **therefore**
  ad. 그러므로, 그것(이것)에 의하여, 그 결과
- **wondering**
  이상히 여기는, 이상한 듯한, 경탄하는

Section 2 Grammar

① Future Time Expressions

When you are meeting clients and customers you will mostly use the present and future tense. Business is usually focused on what happens now, and the future profit. That makes future time expressions very important. Practice your pronunciation of the words listed below.

- today
- this morning/afternoon
- this evening
- tonight
- soon
- later
- around noon
- around midnight
- this Monday
- next Tuesday/next week
- tomorrow afternoon/morning
- in two weeks/two weeks later
- in a few minutes
- in the future
- in two days
- after dinner
- after lunch
- in a while

Section 3 Conversation 1 – Meeting for Coffee

① Try this conversation together with your partner.

Jim	Good morning, Mr. Johnson.
Rick	Good morning, Jim.
Jim	I was in the neighborhood and was wondering if you would like to join me for a cup of coffee.
Rick	That's a great idea, Jim. I'd love to have a coffee with you.
Jim	Ok then, can you meet me in the lobby in about 5 minutes?
Rick	Sure thing. I'll see you then.

Jim	안녕하세요. 미스터 존슨.
Rick	안녕하세요. 짐.
Jim	이웃에 사는 김에 나와 함께 커피나 한 잔 하는 게 어떨지.
Rick	그것 좋은 생각이군요. 짐. 당신과 함께 커피를 마시고 싶습니다.
Jim	좋아요 그러면. 약 5분 뒤에 로비에서 만날까요?
Rick	그럼요. 그때 뵙지요.

Section 4 Exercise 1

① Answer the questions using a future time expression.

1. When will you finish school today?

____

2. What do you want to be in the future?

____

3. What are you going to do after dinner?

____

4. When will you take your vacation?

____

5. When will you meet your friends?

____

Section 5 Conversation 2 – Meeting Clients for Dinner

1 Try this conversation together with your partner.

Brad	Good evening, gentlemen.
Daniel	Brad, it's good to see you again.
Brad	It's good to see you, too. I'm going to take you gentlemen out for dinner. How about a steak and some drinks?
Daniel	That sounds great. Is the restaurant near here?
Brad	It's just down the street. I think you gentlemen will like it.
Daniel	Ok, let's go.

Brad	안녕하세요?
Daniel	브래드, 다시 만나게 돼서 반갑군요.
Brad	다시 만나게 돼서 또한 반갑군요. 저녁식사를 하러 당신을 데리고 나가려던 참입니다. 스테이크와 약간의 음료가 어떠세요?
Daniel	좋군요. 여기 가까이에 레스토랑이 있어요?
Brad	중심거리에 있어요. 당신은 좋아하리라 생각합니다.
Daniel	좋아요, 갑시다.

Section 6 **Exercise 2**

① Write answers for the following questions.

1. Are you having a busy day?

2. What are you working on these days?

3. How is your work coming along?

4. When are you finishing today?

5. Where is your office located?

Section 7 Reading

Drinking Culture

Korea is certainly well known for its drinking and night life. Therefore you should remember that drinking cultures are sometimes different. Koreans for example often drink quickly over a few hours. Many English speaking foreigners drink more slowly but over a longer period of time, sometimes several hours. Both Koreans and foreigners follow these drinking styles without ever thinking about it. Remembering this simple fact can help you adjust your time and speed to better fit the atmosphere and have a good time.

음주 문화

한국은 분명히 음주와 야간 생활로 잘 알려져 있다. 그러므로 당신은 음주 문화가 때때로 다르다는 것을 기억해야 한다. 한국인들은 예컨대 짧은 시간 동안 빠르게 술을 마신다. 많은 영어를 말하는 외국인들은 보다 천천히 마시지만 오랜 시간 동안, 때때로 여러 시간 동안 마신다. 한국인들과 외국인들 모두는 그것에 대해 별로 깊게 생각하지 않고 이러한 음주 유형을 따른다. 이러한 단순한 사실을 기억함으로써 당신은 주위 환경에 보다 잘 적응하는 데 시간과 속도를 조정할 수 있고 또 좋은 시간을 가질 수 있게 된다.

1 Talk to your partner and answer the following questions.

1. Do you like drinking?
2. What do you like to drink?
3. Where do you like drinking: bar, home, pub, nightclub, restaurant, soju tent?
4. What is the drinking age in Korea?
5. Is drinking important for business?
6. Is it Ok to refuse to drink alcohol?

Section 8 Review

1 Find the mistakes and rewrite the sentences.

1. The meeting will be held Tuesday next.

2. The restaurant has a atmosphere very nice.

3. I am going find to a better job soon.

4. I will meet him noon at for lunch

5. The clients will be arriving afternoon tomorrow.

Section 9

Conversation 3 – Golf Meeting

① Try the conversation with your partner.

Mr. Gracie	Hello Mr. Park. How are things with you?
Mr. Park	Things are going well. What can I do for you Mr. Gracie?
Mr. Gracie	Next month on Saturday the 17th my company will be sponsoring a charity golf tournament. Since you are one of our best customers and I know you like to play golf, I was wondering if you would like to join us?
Mr. Park	That sounds wonderful. Where is the tournament taking place?
Mr. Gracie	It's happening at the Sea View Golf and Country Club. The event starts at 10:00 am. There will be prizes, free food and drinks, free caddy and so forth. Can you make it?
Mr. Park	Absolutely, I'd love to attend. The Sea View is one of my favorite golf courses. It would also be a good chance for us to talk about renewing our contract with your company.

Mr. Gracie	안녕하세요. Mr. Park. 하시는 일은 잘 되어 가나요?
Mr. Park	모든 것이 잘 되고 있어요. 뭘 도와드릴까요, Mr. Gracie?
Mr. Gracie	다음달 17일 토요일에 당사는 자선 골프대회를 후원할 것입니다. 귀하는 우리의 우수고객들 중 한 분인데다 골프를 좋아하시는 걸 알고 있기 때문에, 저희와 자리를 함께 하실 생각이 있으신가요?
Mr. Park	정말 좋군요. 경기는 어디에서 개최됩니까?
Mr. Gracie	Sea View Golf 컨트리 클럽에서 개최됩니다. 행사는 오전 10시에 시작합니다. 경품, 무료 음식물, 무료 캐디 등등이 있을 겁니다. 오실 수 있으세요?
Mr. Park	그럼요, 참가하고 싶습니다. Sea View는 제가 좋아하는 골프코스 중의 하나이거든요. 또한 귀사와 계약갱신에 관해 얘기하기에 좋은 기회가 될 것입니다.

2 Ask your partner about the details in the previous conversation.

1. Who is paying for the golf tournament?

2. What is the location of this golf tournament?

3. When is the golf tournament taking place?

4. What does Mr. Park think of the Sea View Golf and Country Club?

5. Why does Mr. Park want to attend the golf tournament?

6. Why did Mr. Gracie invite Mr. Park to play golf?

– 저자약력 –

Trevor B. Mitchell

Trevor B. Mitchell has a Master of Adult Education and a B.A. from St. Francis Xavier University in Antigonish, Nova Scotia, Canada. He also holds a Bachelor of University Studies in education from the University of Maine at Fort Kent, USA. Trevor has taught English in Korea since 1997. He has worked as a business English professor at Ewha Women's University from 2000-2006, and since then continues to teach English for the Department of Management at Dongyang Mirae University in Seoul. His research interests include curriculum and program evaluation.

Baek Ju Hyun

Baek Ju Hyun received his Ph.D. in management from Korea University in Seoul, Korea. He received a special certificate for the Management and Business English program from San Diego State University, USA. He currently teaches Economics, International Business and Business English at Dongyang Mirae University in Seoul, Korea. His research interests include Internatinal Economics and Business.

Stephen L. Poirier

Stephen Poirier completed his Master of Arts in History at the University of Western Ontario in London, Ontario, Canada. He has also received a Certificate of Professional Technical Writing from Carlton University, Ottawa, Ontario, Canada. Stephen has been teaching English since 1992 in Korea, Russia, and Canada. In addition, he spent two years as a history professor at St. Mary's University in Halifax, Nova Scotia, Canada. Stephen currently lives and works in Seoul, Korea.

Basic Business English 2nd Edition

2010년 3월 15일 1판 1쇄 발행
2023년 3월 20일 2판 2쇄 발행

저　　자 | Trevor B. Mitchell · Baek Ju Hyun · Stephen L. Poirier
발 행 인 | 이수영
발 행 처 | 도서출판 청람
서울시 마포구 독막로 288(대흥동, 세양상가 109호)
전　　화 | 02)3272-2601~2
팩　　스 | 02)3272-2603
이 메 일 | crbooks@daum.net
홈페이지 | www.crbooks.co.kr
등　　록 | 2000년 8월 26일 제6-0509호

ISBN 978-89-5972-565-6　93740　[정가 15,000원]